MURDER FOR HIRE PLOTS: OREGON

Margaret LaPlante

AMERICA THROUGH TIME®
ADDING COLOR TO AMERICAN HISTORY

America Through Time is an imprint of Fonthill Media LLC
www.through-time.com
office@through-time.com

Published by Arcadia Publishing by arrangement with Fonthill Media LLC
For all general information, please contact Arcadia Publishing:
Telephone: 843-853-2070
Fax: 843-853-0044
E-mail: sales@arcadiapublishing.com
For customer service and orders:
Toll-Free 1-888-313-2665

www.arcadiapublishing.com

First published 2023

ISBN 978-1-63499-437-8

Typeset in 10pt on13pt Sabon
Printed and bound in England

Contents

Introduction

Murder for hire plots, conspiracy to commit murder, and contract killings may seem like something that only happens in the Mafia, but Oregon has had more than its fair share of these cases. Within the pages of this book are some of the most egregious murder for hire plots that have occurred in Oregon in the past fifty years, including a woman who killed the hitman her husband hired to kill her; the execution-style murder of two adults and two young children; a family who was placed in protective custody due to a contract on their lives; a woman who hired two hitmen to wire her husband's car with dynamite; the contract killings for two police detectives; the murder for hire of a young mother; and the conspiracy to kill the U.S. attorney for the district of Oregon.

1

A Hit on a Hitman

"This is real Chicago gangland stuff" is how the Portland Police Bureau described the killing of Carlos Mendoza in April 1968. Police responded to a call for a man slumped over the front seat of a car that was parked on a dirt road near the Portland International Airport. They arrived on scene and quickly determined that Carlos, age thirty-five, had been shot in the head six times at close range with a small-caliber pistol. The police discovered that the car had been stolen. The investigators did not believe that Carlos had been murdered in the car, but instead had been killed somewhere else and then dumped in the stolen car.

Carlos, who had been a professional boxer, was no stranger to the criminal justice system. He had been convicted of rape, robbery, larceny, and assault. The police knew him from previous investigations into drugs, prostitution, and underworld connections. Carlos had served time at the McNeil Island Federal Prison in Washington.

The Multnomah County grand jury returned secret indictments against Dennis Lee Kniss, age twenty-nine; Benjamin Lonzo Willis, age twenty-four; and Vincent Louis Capitan, age thirty-nine. On October 1, 1968, all three men were arrested. All three men were living in Portland at the time of the murder and were booked into the Rocky Butte Jail in Multnomah County.

Vincent entered a plea of innocent to the charge of murdering Carlos. During the hearing, details emerged claiming that Carlos planned to extort money from Vincent. The threat was that if Vincent did not pay Carlos, then Carlos would testify against him in Vincent's upcoming trial for larceny.

Vincent's trial for larceny got underway. Two people who testified on behalf of Vincent during his larceny trial found themselves on the wrong side of the law; Doris Hildenbrand and David Bryan were charged with false swearing and fined $300. Vincent was convicted of being a habitual criminal stemming from the larceny charge in Yamhill County. Yamhill County Circuit Judge Darrell Williams sentenced Vincent to twenty years in prison for being a habitual criminal; he received this lengthy sentence even without Carlos testifying against him. Although Judge Bryson could have allowed Vincent to remain in Multnomah County jail until his upcoming murder trial was over, he ordered that Vincent begin serving his twenty-year sentence at Oregon State Penitentiary. He explained that once the murder trial began, he would have Vincent transferred to the county jail so he could attend the trial.

The day before the murder trial was to begin, the charges against Vincent's two co-defendants—Benjamin and Dennis—were dismissed. A witness recanted his grand jury testimony linking Benjamin and Dennis to the murder. Judge Bryson granted Vincent attorney's request for a delay due to the new circumstances.

On the morning of October 28, 1969, the murder trial began with Judge Phillip J. Roth presiding. Newspapers across the country covered the details of the trial. Every headline described what they referred to as the "Underworld Trial."

The chief trial counsel for the state attorney general was Thomas D. Odell. He asked the potential members of the jury if they could put aside the fact that many of the witnesses who were going to testify were drug addicts and proven liars. The defense attorney was Oscar D. Howlett, who asked the potential members of the jury if they would be opposed to witnesses who were members of the underworld.

The jury was made up of six men and six women. Thomas told the jury that Vincent murdered Carlos to keep him from testifying at his larceny trial. He explained that Vincent ordered two men to pick up Carlos, drive him out to the airport, and murder him. He admitted that the evidence in the case was only circumstantial. He said that he might not be able to prove that Vincent pulled the trigger but that "he was an accomplice or conspirator to that end."

Oscar wasted no time in telling the jury that Carlos had been arrested seventy-seven times, had beaten one girl to death, and raped another girl. Oscar told the jury, "There was a lot of motive for a lot of people to kill Carlos Mendoza."

The prosecution called Leslie Des Brisay, a Portland bail bondsman, to the stand. Leslie told the court that Carlos had been subpoenaed months before the murder to testify against Vincent in his larceny case. Leslie said that Carlos "seemed pleased at the prospect of testifying if Capitan didn't pay." Vincent's defense attorney objected to Des Brisay's testimony, claiming it was hearsay and opinion only.

The prosecution called Edward Mark Harris to the stand. Edward was charged with being an accessory after the fact. Edward testified that Vincent's stepson, Michael John Wright, and "another man" picked up Carlos at his house and murdered him. It was Edward's testimony that Vincent paid Benjamin Willis $2,500 after the murder took place. According to Edward, the payoff took place at the Willis home. However, Mrs. Willis testified the transaction never took place.

The prosecution put Janet Sherman on the stand. She testified that Vincent told her he was going to kill Carlos. The defense called a fellow inmate of Vincent's to the stand to counter Janet's testimony. Jerome R. Tichenor wasted no time in saying, "she's a liar." Another inmate, Gerald Thompson, testified that Edward Harris confessed to him that he had killed Carlos under the protection of Multnomah County Detective Orlando Yazzolino.

After Edward's testimony, a secret indictment was handed down for Vincent's stepson, Michael age twenty-two, who the prosecution alleged was the shooter. At the time of the indictment, they were unable to locate Michael.

The prosecution called Multnomah County Detective Orlando Yazzolino to the stand. He testified that Vincent had told him that he and Michael were together on the night of the murder. He told the court that when he mentioned that Michael's name had come up in the investigation, Vincent "got extremely excited and said, 'he couldn't have done it—that's my stepson—he's too young.'"

Katherine Drewick took the stand and said she saw the car that Carlos was killed in, parked near Carlos' house the night of his murder. She described to the jury that she saw "a man at the wheel. He was a large man."

While the trial was still underway, the jail staff found Vincent with a gash on his arm. They concluded he had found a piece of tin and made an attempt on his life. Sergeant Robert Smith said, "it wasn't a very serious suicide attempt." Vincent was treated at the Multnomah County Hospital, then returned to his jail cell.

State Medical Examiner Dr. William J. Brady testified about the wounds that Carlos suffered. The prosecution showed the jury the autopsy photos over the objections of the defense. Vincent's girlfriend, Susan Thorne testified on his behalf. She provided Vincent an alibi and claimed he was never involved with the murder of Carlos.

For four weeks, the jury listened to a parade of convicts called to the stand who told stories that could have been made into a movie, but finally the prosecution and defense rested. After six hours of deliberations, the jury found Vincent guilty of murder in the first degree. On the way out of the courtroom, he told reporters, "I wasn't guilty and they found me guilty. It's just too bad." He said he would not appeal, adding, "If the DA's waiting for me to snivel, he's got a long wait." However, his attorney said they would file an appeal. Days after the verdict, Multnomah County Circuit Court Judge Roth sentenced Vincent to life in prison. Vincent stood quietly and did not say a word before being led off under heavy guard.

Vincent had barely settled into his life in prison when Edward Harris was shot to death in a residential section of Boise. The investigators suspected a professional hit. Edward was found slumped in his car with six bullets in his head and throat. The weapon used was a small-caliber pistol. This was all too familiar to the investigators in Portland, as it was exactly the way that Carlos was murdered. Edward had testified in Vincent's trial stating that Michael's stepson and another man were responsible for Carlos' murder.

After learning of Edward's murder, the Multnomah County Sheriff's Office said three people had contracts put out on their lives during Vincent's trial. They listed Edward as one, the others being Detective Orlando Yazzolino and State Attorney Thomas O'Dell. Both Orlando and Thomas were warned that one of the three hits had taken place and that they should be extremely careful. Weeks later, Michael L. Beer, age twenty-one, was arrested for the murder of Edward. Michael had recently been released from a prison in Idaho and was on parole. He was convicted of first-degree murder.

After Vincent's stepson was indicted by the Multnomah County grand jury, a federal warrant was issued for his arrest. Two years later, the F.B.I. located Michael Wright working at a television repair shop in Utah. He was charged with the murder of Carlos Mendoza and interstate flight to avoid prosecution. Michael Wright was brought back to Oregon to stand trial, where he was convicted of first-degree murder.

Vincent's attorney filed an appeal claiming that three of the witnesses who testified during his trial committed perjury. The court ruled against Vincent, saying that he had suborned perjury and therefore the evidence of the perjury convictions was admissible.

Prison authorities became aware that Vincent was involved in a drug smuggling ring within the prison. They began making plans to transfer Vincent to Leavenworth Federal Penitentiary in Kansas. Vincent fought the move claiming he would lose his good behavior privileges and if he was transferred, his family would not be able to visit him.

He filed a *habeas corpus* petition in Federal Court claiming Oregon State Penitentiary Superintendent Hoyt Cupp wanted to transfer him to Leavenworth as retaliation for what other inmates had said about him.

U.S. District Judge Gus Solomon ruled that Vincent had the right to a hearing based on his objections to the transfer. He stated, "Even the most lowly citizen in America is allowed to have a fair and full hearing." Vincent's attorney, Fedric Merrill, stated:

> Here was Capitan, accused of certain things, but not told what they were—and yet, the burden of proof (at the hearings) was put on the prisoner to show why he should not be accused. This is contrary to all rules of evidence.[1]

A hearing was scheduled before Federal District Judge George Juba. Oregon State Penitentiary Superintendent Cupp testified that he needed to transfer Vincent to Leavenworth due to his drug dealing and "other disruptive behavior." It was Superintendent Cupp's testimony that Vincent was operating a protection ring within the prison.

Vincent took the witness stand and became emotional. He tossed the documents listing the charges against him, calling them "all lies." Vincent was on the verge of tears as he described what prison had been like for him saying, "For sixteen months I've been beaten, spit on, and placed in solitary confinement, and I've had all I can take."[2] Judge Juba had to pause the hearing after Vincent's emotional testimony.

When the hearing resumed, three inmates testified that they requested to be placed in solitary confinement because they feared being killed by the "henchmen" of Vincent's. The next inmate who took the witness stand told the court that Vincent had asked him to kill another inmate. Yet another inmate stated Vincent had been very angry with him when he failed to give him any drugs after he returned from a one-day pass to Portland.

A fellow inmate of Vincent's testified that he transported cocaine, heroin, and Dexedrine between Vincent and other inmates more than 100 times. The inmate told the jury he received nothing in return for transporting the drugs. The inmate also testified that he had seen Vincent pass $1,000 to a correctional officer.

Things were looking worse for Vincent when the next inmate told the court that Vincent became upset with him after learning he had turned a gun over to the prison authorities. Vincent had found the gun in the prison.

When the inmates finished testifying, Vincent once again took the stand. He admitted that he had threatened one of the inmates for spreading false rumors about him, but he had never threatened to kill any of the inmates. He vehemently denied everything the inmates had said. Vincent said he had "never in my life bought, sold or used drugs. I wouldn't know heroin or cocaine if I fell in a barrel of it." He added, that a protection racket "couldn't possibly exist" in the prison. He added, "You'd be liable to get killed if you tried."[3]

Vincent was shown a letter he had written to his wife. In the letter he referred to a hospital technician bringing "stuff" into the prison for him. In the letter he reminded his wife to bring the "acid." When confronted with the letter, Vincent told the court that the "stuff" was just cold medication and that the acid was simply going to be used to try and destroy the cell bars so that he could attempt to escape.

The defense called six past and current inmates to the stand to refute the other inmate's testimony. Each of the inmates testified that Vincent was not involved in dealing drugs nor was he involved in a protection racket. One inmate went so far as to say that Vincent was opposed to drugs, adding, "He used to kind of get on me because I was a junkie."[4]

One witness for the defense said he had been housed at the Washington State Penitentiary with Vincent. He stated he incurred Vincent's wrath when he reported him to the prison authorities for operating a bogus check scheme. At the end of the trial, Judge Juba ruled that Vincent should be transferred to Leavenworth. He allowed the state ten days to file a stay with the 9th U.S. Circuit Court of Appeals.

Vincent's attorneys did file an appeal asking that Judge Juba's opinion be vacated. U.S. District Judge Solomon upheld the ruling that Vincent be transferred out of the Oregon State Penitentiary. He based his opinion on the evidence that was presented during the hearing.

Before he could be transferred, Vincent once again made an attempt on his life. He was being held in the city jail in Salem awaiting the transfer. Vincent knotted together several towels and tied them to the bars of his cell and attempted to hang himself. The jail personnel had a doctor attend to Vincent's injuries, which consisted of a minor head bruise.

After a few years at Leavenworth, Vincent filed a lawsuit in U.S. District Court asking to be returned to Oregon. He argued that the inmates who had accused him of threatening their lives had been released. He was ordered to remain at Leavenworth.

Although Vincent was sentenced to life in prison for the murder of Carlos, the day came that he was released from prison. He walked out of prison in 1980 but it was not the last that law enforcement would hear from him. Four years later, he was in trouble with the U.S. Bureau of Alcohol, Tobacco, and Firearms for being a felon in possession of four guns. Vincent was living in Milwaukie, Oregon, at the time.

In 1981, Vincent married his twenty-two-year-old girlfriend, Linda. Soon after, Vincent and Linda settled outside of Redding, California, in the Lake Shasta area. Vincent was earning a living by gambling in cardrooms in Redding. By 1986, the marriage was fractured. Vincent filed for divorce citing irreconcilable differences. At the time of the divorce proceedings, Vincent and Linda had two young children—a five-year-old girl and a three-year-old boy.

On the evening of February 6, 1987, Vincent was shot to death near his home, outside of Redding in Jones Valley. Vincent was at home waiting for his neighbors to come over to play Trivial Pursuit. He thought he heard prowlers on his property so he went outside to check on his property. He left his children alone in the house. He ended up getting in his car and chasing the prowlers who had fled in their car. At the bottom of the hill, he got out of his car. The minute he exited his car, he was shot just below his heart. The prowlers sped off. Vincent's fifteen-year-old neighbor heard a gunshot, grabbed a flashlight and went out to investigate. He came across Vincent, barely breathing who uttered his last words, "check on my kids." He was fifty-seven years old at the time of his death.

Shasta County Sheriff's Office began their investigation into the murder of Vincent. Detective Sergeants Larry Jarrett and Fred Carelli were assigned to the case. Sergeant Rusty Brewer of the Shasta County Sheriff's Office told reporters with the Associated Press, "We will be doing a lot of interviewing in this area and probably later in Portland, as the investigation progresses."[5]

The first person the investigators looked at was Linda. They learned more details about the relationship. They found out that Linda had walked out on Vincent the previous Father's Day. They had gone out for brunch at the Shasta Inn in Redding. She gave Vincent some presents and things seemed fine. Vincent walked across the street to play poker at the Casino Club. Linda and the children returned home. Linda packed their belongings and most of the furniture and left with the children. Vincent hired private detectives to comb three states trying to find his children. Months later, Linda and the children were located living in an apartment in Chico, California, with Linda's boyfriend. Vincent won custody of the children and they moved to Fort Jones to live with him.

The investigation took a dramatic turn when an anonymous caller came forward with information that Linda had ordered a hit on Vincent. Linda was arrested at her home in Chico and charged with murder and conspiracy to commit murder. After Vincent's murder, the two children had been placed with Linda. As Linda was led off in handcuffs, the children were turned over to Child Protection Services. The children were later placed with Linda's mother. Linda was booked into the Shasta County Jail.

As the investigation wore on, Randy and Michelle Schmoll, who lived outside of Redding, in the town of Anderson, came forward with the information that three acquaintances of theirs from Santa Cruz had appeared uninvited at their home. The three men spent the night at the Schmoll's home but they appeared to be "jumpy" according to their hosts. The Schmolls told the investigators that the men made several calls to Portland in search of money. The Schmolls gave the detectives the names of the three men.

The investigators learned that the three men had driven up Interstate 5 to a truck stop where they received $150 that had been wired to them via Com Check. The sender of the funds was listed as Nancy Kellotat. Next, they learned that the car the suspects had been driving was abandoned at the Portland International Airport. It sat gathering dust with fuzzy dice still dangling from the rearview mirror. Records showed that two of the men had boarded a plane to San Jose and the other flew to San Francisco.

Weeks after Linda was arrested, the police arrested Jody Dean Seelye (A.K.A. Schultz and Vaughn) at a motel in Portland. Jody was believed to be the triggerman. At first, Jody refused to waive extradition to Shasta County, but after a month, he agreed to be transported to the Shasta County Jail.

By the time the authorities had identified another man involved in the contract killing, they learned they were too late. Clarence "Animal" Griffin, age twenty-three, had been killed in an automobile accident after he lost control of his vehicle while driving drunk near Morgan Hill, California. They examined his girlfriend's telephone bill and saw a collect call from Anderson on the night Vincent was murdered.

The investigation led detectives to Jeff McKinney, age twenty-six, who was living in Modesto. Jeff and Jody were former inmates at the Oregon State Penitentiary. The detectives believed that Jody asked Jeff to help him with the murder.

Locating the next two subjects involved in the murder plot required the help of the F.B.I. The detectives identified Nancy Jo Cavataio Kellotat, age forty-two, and her husband, Phillip Kellotat, also age forty-two, as being the people Linda asked to find a hitman to murder her husband. Linda and Nancy had been roommates at one time. Detectives travelled from Shasta County and assisted the Portland Police Bureau when they executed a search warrant on the Kellotat's house in Portland. Following the search, Nancy was arrested for possession of a controlled substance. They did not have enough to charge her with any serious crimes. Phillip was on leave from the Oregon

State Penitentiary. When the police made contact with him, they did not have enough evidence to arrest him.

Nancy was released on bail, and once she was free, she and Phillip disappeared. The police discovered they were gone when they served another search warrant at their home in Portland. The police confiscated twenty-one emeralds, a ruby, several watches, some rings, computer equipment, and $2,024 in cash. They also seized cocaine, instructions for manufacturing drugs, chemicals used to make methamphetamine, and books on how to make fraudulent identification cards. Additionally, they seized blank birth certificates from Oklahoma, an Oklahoma notary seal, and bundles of blank social security cards.

The Shasta County Sheriff's Office continued their work on the case. Once they completed their investigation, warrants were issued for Nancy Jo and Phillip on a charge of murder. With a date for a preliminary hearing fast approaching, the Shasta County Sheriff's Office and Deputy District Attorney Dennis Sheehy requested the help of the F.B.I. in locating the Kellotats.

Phillip manged to evade law enforcement for eight months but was located in Bakersfield, California. His down fall came when he went to the Department of Motor Vehicles (D.M.V.) to register his motorcycle. The D.M.V. determined that he was using a fictious name and notified the Bakersfield Police Department. He was arrested and booked into the Kern County Jail. His fingerprints gave him away and the authorities identified him as Phillip Kellotat. He was held on a no-bail warrant awaiting extradition to Shasta County. After Phillip was arrested, he told the police he and Nancy Jo fled because his wife was accused "of a murder she did not commit." He added he feared his own "rumored involvement" might result in retaliation from the underworld.

At the time of Phillip's arrest, the Bakersfield Police Department confiscated numerous weapons from Phillip including a fully automatic MAC 11 machine gun. They believed Nancy had been with Phillip but their efforts to locate her were futile.

By the time Phillip arrived in Redding, Linda had been cleared of all charges. Although she had been at the heart of the murder for hire plot, the charges against her were dismissed due to a lack of evidence. Her attorney, Russell Schwartz, told the court, "Her position is very simple: she is not guilty of any of the charges or allegations." He added, "Vincent Capitan was an individual with a number of very formidable enemies."[6]

When Phillip was captured, District Attorney Steve Carlton said he had no immediate plans to refile charges against Linda but he emphasized, "If we obtain more evidence in connection with the Linda Capitan case from this arrest, then we will review it and make a decision."[7]

At Phillip's preliminary hearing, he listened to the evidence against him, which led to being charged with murder in the first degree, murder for financial gain, and conspiracy to commit murder. He pled not guilty to all charges. District Attorney Carlton told reporters he was considering seeking the death penalty for Phillip.

Phillip had not been in the Shasta County jail very long when things became even more complicated. His defense attorney, Bernard DePaoli, found himself on the wrong side of the law. He was arrested and charged with attempting to bribe a witness. Alan Bradley was scheduled to testify that Phillip hired him, Dawn Walker, and Jeff McKinney to murder Vincent. Alan had recently been convicted and sentenced to seven years for assault with a deadly weapon for a crime he committed in Humboldt County. Alan was scheduled to testify against Phillip when he was approached by Phillip's defense attorney. Alan told the prison authorities that Bernard paid him $400 after Phillip's preliminary hearing. Alan said there were "vague promises" of additional money. After Shasta County District Attorney Carlton confronted Bernard about the allegations of bribing a witness, he withdrew as Phillip's attorney. He was arrested but was released soon after. A week after his arrest, he requested to be reinstated as Phillip's attorney. His request was granted.

Phillip's trial got underway with Trinity County Judge K. Letton presiding. Shasta County District Attorney Carlton explained to the jury that while serving time in the Oregon State Penitentiary for armed robbery, Phillip put into motion a murder for hire plot against Vincent Capitan. He explained that even though Phillip was behind bars at the time of Vincent's murder, he had been a drug lord prior to going to prison and had many ties with the underworld. District Attorney Carlton told the jury the murder for hire was done as a favor to a friend of Phillip's wife, Linda Capitan. He explained that Linda was in a bitter custody battle with Vincent over their two young children. He went on to say that Linda stood to gain financially from Vincent's life insurance policy.

Both Alan and Dawn testified that Phillip hired them to murder Vincent at his house outside of Redding. Jeff agreed to testify against Phillip in exchange for a lesser sentence. Jeff told the court that he, Jody, and Clarence were hired to murder Vincent. He implicated the Kellotats in the murder plot. He said Jody informed him that Vincent "was a child molester and there was a contract to kill him." It was Jeff's testimony that Jody shot Vincent using a sawed-off shotgun. He added that Jody seemed pleased with how things turned out, "he said it was a good job. He liked it." He admitted under oath to driving the getaway car the night Vincent was killed.

After the trio finished testifying, Bernard argued that the only evidence against his client was the testimony of Alan, Dawn, and Jeff. He emphasized that none of their testimony could be considered truthful.

Jody was scheduled to testify against Phillip, the man he claimed hired him to murder Vincent. The Shasta County District Attorney's Office had offered Jody a new identity and promised he would be placed in an out of state prison if he testified against Phillip. The day before he was to testify, he had a change of heart and decided not to testify at Phillip's trial. He pled guilty to murder in the first degree and murder for financial gain. He admitted he was paid $5,000 to murder Vincent. Judge Donald Kennedy accepted Jody's pleas and set sentencing at a later date.

With the loss of their star witness, the district attorney's office felt they had no choice but to release Phillip. In referring to the turn of events, Deputy District Attorney Sheehy told reporters:

> Jody Seelye was our case against Kellotat. But he changed his mind. Since we didn't have him, we had no reason for going forward. He's reneged on that. He backed out. There is no point in proceeding any further with Kellotat. That's too bad because the real bad guy here is Phil Kellotat. It's a frustrating case. With a couple of breaks, it could have all come together. But now we have less than a storybook ending.[8]

Jody's attorney, Richard Maxion told the reporters, "I feel it is a fair resolution of the case. It was a strong case against him."[9] Jody was sentenced to life in prison without the possibility of parole. By taking the plea, he avoided a possible death sentence.

The Shasta County Sheriff's Office turned Phillip over to the Oregon State Penitentiary where he was wanted for escaping after he failed to return from the day pass when he originally fled Oregon.

It was not long after his release that a new warrant was issued for Phillip. He was charged with murder and murder-for-hire. The warrant was sent to the authorities in Oregon so they could begin preparations for extraditing Phillip back to California.

One year after his first trial, Phillip found himself back in the same courthouse facing charges of murder in the first degree and conspiracy to commit murder, both of which he pled not guilty to. Bernard DePaoli was once again representing him. District Attorney Carlton told the jury:

> Vincent Capitan was gunned down in a murder for hire. It's as simple as that, and everyone knows it ... The only issue is whether or not Phil Kellotat hired Jody Seelye to kill Vince Capitan. Vince Capitan was a human being, and he was entitled, as we all are, not to be murdered.[10]

District Attorney Carlton explained to the jury that even though Phillip was behind bars in Oregon when Vincent was murdered, he was responsible for orchestrating the entire murder for hire. He told the jury that Phillip's criminal record stretched back thirty years to when he was convicted of burglary at the age of thirteen. He had been arrested a total of twenty times as an adult. The crimes included drug use, drug trafficking, and armed robbery. Bernard argued that Vincent was killed due to his involvement in the drug underworld. He told the jury that there were plenty of people in the underworld who wanted to kill Vincent.

This time Jody did testify against Phillip. He told the jury that Phillip hired him to kill Vincent. He explained to the jury that arrangements were made so as soon as Jody was released from the Oregon State Penitentiary, Vincent would be murdered

Alan testified at Phillip's second trial. He explained to the jury that back in 1986, Phillip hired him and his then-girlfriend to kill Vincent. Alan told the court that he traveled from Oregon to California but was unable to locate Vincent. He returned to Oregon and told Phillip that he was not able to complete the hit.

The jury deliberated for two days before returning a verdict of not guilty on all charges. Phillip nodded his head and smiled, then shook hands with Bernard. District Attorney Carlton was visibly upset but told the reporters, "The jury has spoken; we gave it our best shot." In speaking to the reporters about Phillip's trial, Bernard said:

> It proved to me our jury system works. It's too bad our judicial system doesn't work. I think it should have been dismissed a long time ago, and it's a travesty because a man spent a year to a year-and-a-half in custody, and I think we should have won way before this.[11]

Throughout both of Phillip's trials, his wife, Nancy, was still living life on the lam. Phillip's defense attorney, Bernard DePaoli, represented Nancy. He offered to surrender Nancy to the authorities in exchange for "a reasonable bail." Law enforcement rejected his offer and located her on their own. It took two years for the F.B.I. to locate Nancy. She was living in Eureka, California, when they arrested her on a warrant charging her with murder, murder for financial gain, and conspiracy to commit murder.

Bernard was confident that Nancy would be acquitted, just as Phillip was. District Attorney Carlton was just as confident that his case against Nancy was stronger than the case against her husband. Jody told the authorities that Nancy was the go-between for receiving payment in exchange for killing Vincent, and District Attorney Carlton planned to present this to the jury.

As it turned out, Nancy pled guilty to being an accessory to murder. All of the other charges against her were dropped. Nancy was sentenced to three years' probation for her role in the murder of Vincent Capitan. District Attorney Carlton told the reporters:

> Basically, we were able to prove she paid the man who actually did the killing. But she contended that she didn't know about the murder until after it happened. And we knew we'd have difficulty disputing that with evidence.[12]

After Phillip was acquitted on all charges, he admitted to the authorities that he did have Vincent murdered. He could not be tried for the murder, as he had already been acquitted.

The jewelry seized from the Kellotats' home during the second search warrant was auctioned off three years after it was seized. The proceeds from the auction went to Multnomah County.

2

Phillip Kellotat Strikes Again

While being questioned by the detectives in Shasta County about the murder of Vincent, Jody Seelye told of another murder for hire plot that Phillip had orchestrated. According to Jody, Thomas Francis Hyland had been an inmate at the Oregon State Penitentiary at the same time that Phillip was incarcerated.

Thomas had been sentenced to ten years in the Oregon State Penitentiary for robbery and burglary. He escaped in 1986 when he walked away from the prison's farm annex. He was caught and returned to his cell. In March 1987, he was released from prison on temporary leave. According to Jody, in May 1987, Phillip asked him to murder Thomas. At the time, Phillip claimed that Thomas had stolen $4,000 in gold coins.

Jody told the detectives he refused to murder Thomas because he had just killed Vincent three months before. Jody went on to say that Phillip then made arrangements for Dennis Beach to perform the murder for hire. He said Dennis was willing to complete the murder "to clear drug debts owed to Kellotat." Dennis had been sentenced to sixteen years for robbery and kidnapping in Lane County. He began serving his sentence at the Oregon State Correctional Institution in April 1980. In 1983, he was transferred to the Oregon State Penitentiary where he came in contact with Phillip. Dennis managed to escape twice in two years by walking away from job details.

Jody described to the investigators exactly how the murder took place. He said, "Dennis said that he shot Tommy in the leg and then shot him in the head, and then he threw a cardboard box over him and then shot him again."[1] Jody told the detectives that Thomas' body could be found near Brownsville, outside of Albany.

Detectives in Shasta County contacted the Linn County Sheriff's Office to inform them of what Jody told them about a murder that may have taken place in their jurisdiction. Linn County Sheriff's Office sent out a search party to try and find the remains of Thomas, but, in the end, they were unsuccessful.

Later, a group of hikers came across skeletal remains and some clothing in a wooded area southeast of Holley. A dentist identified the remains as that of Thomas Francis Hyland. Detectives from the Linn County Sheriff's Office notified Thomas' sister in Ohio. The state medical examiner in Portland was tasked with determining how Thomas was killed.

Investigators with the Linn County Sheriff's Office contacted the Shasta County Sheriff's Office after locating the remains. After Jody's statement was read to Lieutenant Holm, he stated, "there is evidence of that happening."

Detectives from Linn County Sheriff's Office traveled to Shasta County to talk with the investigators who worked the Vincent Capitan murder for hire case. Afterwards, Lieutenant Holm said, "We have a lot more information on this case than on most bodies we find after a couple of years."[2] Lieutenant Dar Holm with the Linn County Sheriff's Office told reporters:

> We spent a lot of time and money, but it's a big county with a lot of rough terrain. The body was well hidden and wouldn't have been discovered where it was except animals had been dragging out some of the pieces.[3]

Dennis was never tried for Thomas' murder. He was shot while trying to retrieve his cattle from a relative's property. The shooting occurred in a remote area of Oregon north of Enterprise near the Blue Mountains. A relative of Dennis,' Donna Beach Dunning, was sentenced to seven years in prison for his death. The family had roots in the Wallowa County's ranching industry for more than a century.

3

Shelly Miller

At 9 p.m. on February 22, 1982, Shelly Miller finished her shift working in the shoe department at the Meier and Frank Department Store in Salem. She was anxious to get home to her six-month-old son, Douglas, Jr., and her husband, Douglas, Sr.

When Shelly did not return home from work, her husband phoned the Marion County Sheriff's Office just after midnight to report his wife missing. The next morning at about 9 a.m., he called the Marion County Sheriff's Office again to say that he and a friend had located his wife. He told the police that she had been murdered in her car, which was parked less than a mile from their home.

The deputies arrived at the crime scene and located Shelly slumped in the front seat of her car. She had been shot in the left temple. The Salem Police Department told reporters that they did not have a suspect or a motive at that time. Shelly's purse was still inside her light blue Audi Fox, leading police to believe that robbery was not the motive. Sergeant Larry Stephens of the Salem Police Department asked the public to contact him if they had any information.

Although the police did not want to give any specific information to the public about the murder, Douglas told reporters that one shell casing had been located in the car. He explained why he reported her missing by saying, "Shelly was a very reliable person. In the event she was going to be late, she would always call someone." Douglas said Shelly had a cold that day but went to work for the last part of her shift. He said he last spoke to his wife at about 8 p.m. while she was at work. He said she was "in the greatest of spirits." Douglas said he stayed up all night worrying and the next day he and a friend drove around looking for Shelly's car. When he found it, he said, "As soon as I pulled in there, I knew there was something wrong."[1] He said there was a party planned for her birthday and he had been told by one of her co-workers that she was bringing home a box of candy for the party.

Shelly was born in Seattle. In 1971, the family moved to Salem. She graduated from McNary High School in 1977. In her senior year, she was nominated for the homecoming court. She had been working for Meier and Frank since she was sixteen years old. Shelly and Douglas married in 1978. Douglas had a daughter from a previous marriage. Shelly was one day shy of her twenty-third birthday at the time of her death. In addition to her husband and baby, she was survived by her parents, Webster and Joan Terwilliger; her brothers, Shane and Kelley Terwilliger; and her sister, Shawnee Comer.

Shelly's friends described her as outgoing and well-liked. They said she worshipped her baby, Douglas, Jr., who went by the name of D.J. They said she was in seventh heaven with her newborn baby. The comments about Shelly included: "She was the sweetest person in the world. She would have done anything for anybody."

Medical Examiner William Brady performed an autopsy of the body on the day of Shelly's twenty-third birthday. He told the *Statesman Journal*, "I'm confident we're going to have a resolution on this reasonably soon."

The neighboring stores reevaluated their safety practices. Representatives from nearby Nordstrom, JCPenney, Frederick and Nelson, and PayLess told reporters from the *Statesman Journal* that their employees left the stores together but it was still a potentially dangerous situation. Nordstrom put on a self-protection class for their employees after learning of Shelly's murder.

Two weeks after Shelly was found in her car, the police arrested Jeffrey Lee Allen, age twenty-one. Jeffrey was a mechanic by trade. He had recently moved to Salem from Tracy, California. Jeffrey was arrested for hindering prosecution in this case. The Salem Police Department and the Marion County District Attorney's Office believed that Jeffrey was the person who shot Shelly. Then, on March 12, 1982, Shelly's husband, Douglas Ray Miller, age twenty-seven, was arrested on a charge of aggravated murder. The detectives believed Douglas hired Jeffrey to kill his wife.

On March 18, 1982, Douglas appeared before Marion County Circuit Court Judge Richard D. Barber and pled innocent to a charge of aggravated murder. He was represented by defense attorney Charles Burt. Before the hearing was finished, Deputy District Attorney Dick Scruggs asked the court to declare Marvin Glen Miller (no relation to Douglas) and Howard Thomas Allen, Jeffrey's uncle, material witnesses. Based on the investigation, Deputy District Attorney Scruggs explained that after interviewing numerous sources, he believed that Douglas first tried to hire Howard Allen and Marvin Miller to kill Shelly. Judge Barber granted the request. He authorized the men to be released on their own recognizance with the caveat that the men keep the investigators apprised of their whereabouts. He stressed that they could not leave the state of Oregon without his permission.

Details began to emerge regarding two life insurance policies that the couple took out after the baby was born. Each policy was worth $150,000 and would be paid to the surviving spouse and child.

Five weeks after Shelly was murdered, Jeffrey pled guilty to a charge of murder. He told Judge Barber, "I inflicted the gunshot wound that killed Shelly Miller." Jeffrey accepted a plea agreement wherein he pled guilty in exchange for testifying at Douglas' trial. By doing so, he was told he would be eligible for parole at the earliest date possible under the state parole board's matrix system. Jeffrey was still facing a sentence of life in prison, but because of the plea agreement, there would not be a minimum time that he had to serve prior to being released. However, Douglas was facing a life sentence with a minimum of thirty years before he would be eligible for parole.

Deputy District Attorney Scruggs told Judge Barber, "Mr. Allen's cooperation included providing information leading to the seizure of the weapon involved and the identity of the principal actor in the conspiracy, as well as the identities of other co-conspirators." He went onto explain that when Jeffrey came forward with the information, he was not in custody and was not considered criminally involved with the murder. Deputy District Attorney Scruggs said that Jeffrey "was the first person to expose the conspiracy to kill Shelly Miller to law enforcement officers."[2] The plea agreement was approved by Jeffrey's court-appointed defense attorney Timothy B. O'Neill as well as Shelly's parents. Judge Barber said that he would take the plea agreement under advisement.

The following week, Judge Barber ruled that he would accept Jeffrey's plea agreement. He postponed the sentencing hearing until after Douglas' trial to make sure that Jeffrey followed through on testifying at that trial.

The next ruling Judge Barber needed to make involved whether or not he would allow Douglas to be released on bail. The courtroom was cleared before the bailiff brought Douglas into the courtroom. Those wanting to be present at the bail hearing had to be searched before being allowed back into the courtroom. Deputy District Attorney Michael Brown argued that there was enough evidence to suggest that Douglas was involved in his wife's death to deny bail. Charles argued that Jeffrey was not a credible witness, therefore his testimony should not be considered. Charles added, "The court has to realize that this man is a co-conspirator. He's an accomplice." Judge Barber ruled that there was sufficient evidence to deny Douglas' request for bail.

Shelly's father, Webster, was appointed to represent her estate in probate court. Upon learning of this, Douglas had his father file documents contesting the appointment. Douglas argued in the documents that either he, or his nominee, the Commercial Bank of Salem, should be the representative of his wife's estate, which was valued at $15,000.

The grand jury indicted Jeffrey's uncle, Howard Allen, on charges of solicited murder and aggravated murder. The grand jury based that on Jeffrey's affidavit that read in part, "Howard Allen solicited me on behalf of Douglas Ray Miller to murder Shelly Miller. Howard Allen informed me that I would be paid by Douglas Ray Miller if I would murder Shelly Miller." Howard was arrested and lodged at the county jail. Howard's attorneys argued that he should be granted bail because he did not have a criminal history and the evidence against him was weak. The judge ruled against allowing Howard out on bail.

Five months to the day that Shelly's body was discovered, Douglas' trial got underway with Judge Clarke Brown presiding. The jury was made up of five men and seven women, with two male alternates. Deputy District Attorney Scruggs began his opening statements by stating that Douglas had made four previous attempts to have his wife murdered before she was killed on February 22, 1982. Charles began his opening statements by laying out a defense that Shelly's murder was the result of a drug deal gone wrong.

District Attorney Scruggs laid out the case saying that Jeffrey had been paid $10,000 to kill Shelly. He took the jury through the life insurance policies that the couple had purchased. He stressed that Shelly's policy had a double indemnity clause that would pay out $300,000 if she died of something other than natural causes. The district attorney said that as soon as that policy was approved in late January, Douglas began making arrangements to have his wife murdered. He said that Douglas contacted Jeffrey's uncle, Howard Allen, and set the plan in motion. Douglas gave Jeffrey directions as to how he wanted the murder to take place. It was District Attorney Scruggs' statement that the first time Jeffrey was supposed to commit the murder, he changed his mind and went to a party instead.

When the first attempt was a failure, Douglas next gave Jeffrey a map of the parking lot of the Meier and Frank store. They allegedly studied the map and then drove to the store one night when Shelly was working. Douglas provided Jeffrey with a spare key to Shelly's car. According to District Attorney Scruggs, Jeffrey unlocked the car, but got cold feet and backed out. Days later, they attempted this scenario again, but again, Jeffrey backed out. The fourth attempt, said District Attorney Scruggs, was when Douglas hired a babysitter to look after their infant so he could get Shelly away from the house and Jeffrey could complete the murder. This plan went awry when the babysitter cancelled at the last minute.

District Attorney Scruggs told the jury that on the night Shelly died, Douglas called her at work and requested that on her way home, she stop off at the Oregon Acceptance Company and drop off a payment through their night deposit slot. He said that Jeffrey drove to the Oregon Acceptance Company, parked his car nearby, and was hiding in the bushes when Shelly arrived. Jeffrey had borrowed a gun from his aunt and he forced Shelly, at gunpoint, to drive to a nearby park where he shot her behind the ear.

Charles laid out a completely different scenario. He told the jury the Millers were financially stable and had nothing more than "garden-variety" marital problems. He explained that they paid their bills in cash or used a cashier's check, but they did not have a bank account. Charles questioned if Jeffrey had unlocked her car on two occasions when she was at work, why she never mentioned it to anyone. He explained that the couple had recently purchased a spa and were making monthly payments on it. Charles brought up the point that Shelly would not have had the payment book with her and therefore could not stop off on her way home and make a payment at the Oregon Acceptance Company.

As Charles continued his opening statements, he said that although Shelly was not known to use drugs, her husband "wasn't that smart." He went on to say that Douglas knew "big-time drug dealers and the muscle that goes with it." Charles told the court that Douglas had been involved in some large-scale drug deals that resulted in someone stealing $40,000 worth of drugs. Charles said that Douglas had received death threats against his family due to his involvement with these people. Charles turned to the jury and asked, "Isn't it interesting his wife was executed gangland style by someone in that drug culture?"

Shelly's father, Webster, testified that Shelly and Douglas' marriage problems were more than "garden-variety." He said Shelly was committed to the marriage and wanted it to work. He said, "Before she had been so positive about making the marriage work." Webster said about a month before she was killed, he noticed a change, as though she had given up hope that the marriage would survive.

Shelly's cousin, Laurie Lynn Johnson, also testified that the marriage was "going downhill." Laurie added, "She was very depressed. She wanted to make it work, but she wasn't going to stick around if it didn't." Laurie said that Shelly had brought the baby to visit her in Seattle two weeks before her death. Referring to the marriage, Laurie said, "She wanted to make it work. She had planned to give it one last try. If it didn't work, she planned on coming back to Seattle." Laurie told the court that the marriage problems revolved around a lack of communication, sharing responsibilities, and Douglas' lack of respect for Shelly. Laurie spoke of their disagreement about Shelly returning to work after D.J. was born. She said, "She wasn't really interested in going back to work. She didn't feel she should leave the baby at such a young age."[3] Laurie confirmed that Shelly agreed to work part time. She told the court that Shelly and Douglas had moved to Seattle the previous year but returned to Salem after four months. She said Shelly told her if Douglas did not agree to see a marriage counselor by the beginning of March, she was going to move back to Seattle.

Douglas' friend Jerry Frunz took the stand and described an entirely different marriage. He said he only knew of one argument between the couple. He said after that argument, Shelly spent two nights at his house with his wife. Jerry said Shelly "would do anything for Doug." Jerry walked the jury through his contact with Douglas the night of the crime. He said he received a phone call from Douglas about 10:30 p.m.; Douglas explained that Shelly had not returned home from work. Jerry said Douglas had already asked one of his relatives to drive around and look for Shelly's car. He said he went to the Miller house and then he and Douglas drove around for a while looking for her car. He added that they drove past the Fred Meyer store because, "Doug said she was going to stop at Fred Meyer to get some cold medicine."

Jerry testified that after they drove around, they returned to the Miller's residence and called law enforcement. He said a deputy from the Marion County Sheriff's Office arrived and took the missing person's report. Jerry said the deputy told Douglas to remain at home, so he went out alone and looked for Shelly. At 1:30 a.m., he returned to the Miller's residence and fell asleep. The next morning, he and Douglas, went out again in search of Shelly's car. It was then, he said, they located Shelly dead from a gunshot wound slumped in the front seat of her car. From time to time during Jerry's testimony, Douglas looked teary eyed and put a handkerchief to his eyes.

The jurors listened to the tape recording of Douglas' call to the Marion County Sheriff's Office at 12:02 a.m. on February 23, 1982. In that call, Douglas asked if there had been any traffic accidents. When the answer was negative, he stated he needed to report his wife missing. Another tape recording was played. This recording was prior to the one where Douglas reported his wife missing. On this particular recording, Douglas did not identify himself; he simply asked if there had been any traffic accidents.

Glen Miller told the court that he had been approached by Douglas several times asking him to find someone to "take care of" his wife. He explained that he and Douglas were close friends and that Douglas had confided, "he was getting tired of her [Shelly] badmouthing him. He asked if I knew of somebody who could take care of somebody." Glen said he asked Douglas who the intended victim was, and Douglas told him it was his wife. Glen told the court, "I was totally shocked. I thought he was kidding around."[4]

Despite this, Glen provided Douglas with the names of two potential hitmen, "who had the reputation for being pretty bad." Glen said they went to the home of one of the men and the three of them sat in Douglas' car and talked about the possible hit on Shelly. Glen said that Douglas offered the man $10,000–$15,000 from the life insurance proceeds, but that he did not want Shelly touched or raped. Glen remembered the man saying, "he didn't want no part of it." However, the potential hitman did say, "there might be somebody in the house that might do it," referring to one of his roommates.[5]

According to Glen, Douglas called the roommate the following day, but the deal fell through. He once again asked Glen for names of potential hitmen. Glen gave him the name of one more potential subject. They drove to the man's house but the man laughed at the proposal and they left without securing a hitman.

After striking out with three potential hitmen, Douglas once again asked Glen if he would take care of Shelly. Glen told the court, "Two or three days later he asked if I would do it. I said no, there ain't no way I could do something like that."[6] The following week, Douglas informed him that he had spoken to a potential hitman and it looked promising. Glen reiterated to the court that he did not take Douglas seriously when he spoke of having his wife killed.

Nevertheless, Glen was introduced to the potential hitman the week before Shelly was murdered. The man gave his name as "Bob." Glen said he later learned that the man was Jeffrey Allen. Glen said that on the night of Shelly's murder, Douglas invited him to his house. He recalled arriving about 8:45 p.m. Glen said when he began preparing to leave, "Doug said he wanted me to stay a little longer. He said he had a funny feeling about whether Shelly was going to make it home or not. Glen added, I just wanted to get out of there."[7]

At this point in Glen's testimony, Deputy District Attorney Brown asked Glen if he was becoming suspicious. Glen admitted that he was "a little bit" suspicious at the time. Glen testified that days after Shelly was killed, Doug took him aside and "said he didn't know who did it, and he had nothing to do with it." When asked if he believed Douglas, Glen admitted he did not.

Three insurance professionals took the stand and described in detail how the life insurance policies worked. The jury learned that Douglas and Shelly took out a joint whole life insurance policy two years prior to Shelly's death. Next, they took out separate convertible-term policies worth $150,000 each. They also acquired a $39,000 decreasing-term mortgage insurance policy five weeks before the murder. Allstate Insurance Agent Cyrus Gladen explained that Shelly's policy had a double-indemnity value of $300,000 in the event that she died from something other than natural causes. He added that the couple wanted to spend the same amount for each policy, but the policy for women cost less, so they increased the amount of coverage which made the premiums the same price. Cyrus told the jury that originally Shelly's policy was only worth $100,000 as that was standard practice until the underwriter approved the policy. Cyrus said that the underwriter had approved the policy less than six weeks before she was killed thus increasing the policy to $150,000.

All eyes were on Carol Cutter as she made her way to the witness stand. Rumors had been circulating that Douglas had been cheating on Shelly. Carol admitted that she and Douglas had sex a year before and again two weeks before Shelly was murdered. She told the court Shelly was in Washington visiting relatives when she met up with Douglas the second week of February. When asked if there was a relationship between the two, she stated, "No promises were made about any type of relationship. He said he might call me ... and I had a feeling he might call me."[8] Carol admitted she was married at the time she had an affair with Douglas, adding that she was currently in divorce proceedings.

William W. Davis took the stand and explained that he was a marriage counselor and Shelly and Douglas had been clients of his. He said they first came to see him in October 1980. He went on to explain that he saw them six times before they moved to Seattle in March 1981. He said that Shelly was the one who contacted his office with concerns about her marriage. William said Shelly was committed to making the marriage work and that before they left for Seattle, she was "feeling better about the marriage. There was more openness, and her trust level was improving." William encouraged them to find a counselor in Seattle and continue working on the relationship, adding, "We had Band Aided the situation, but it really was not finished." William told the court the next time he heard from Shelly was six days before she was killed. He described her as "emotionally fatigued with not much coping energy left. She was depressed, really down, compared to the bright, energetic, bubbly person I had been used to the year before. She felt she had done everything she thought she could do for the marriage." William said that Shelly was feeling insecure and was concerned as to why Douglas was being secretive about his business dealings. William added, "It was a frightening situation for her."[9]

In his opening statements, Charles had opened the door for a possible defense due to a drug deal gone wrong. Brad Nevell took the stand and told the court that he had been involved in selling and using drugs since high school. Brad said he knew Shelly in high school and remembered, "She was a real nice, sweet lady. If she had any enemies, I sure wasn't aware of it." He adamantly denied that his drug dealings had anything to do with Shelly's murder. Brad said he was an acquaintance of Douglas. He said at the beginning of February, he received a phone call from Glen Miller who asked if he wanted to make $25,000. Brad said he indicated he was interested so they made arrangements to meet, but when Brad got to the meeting, he was surprised to see Douglas there. Brad recalled Douglas stating he "wanted somebody taken care of." When Brad asked Douglas, if he wanted someone hurt, he replied, "No, I want 'em killed."

Brad told the court, "I didn't know him in this capacity at all, so I was kind of shocked. I asked who, and he said Shelly. I asked him why, and he said an insurance policy." This took Brad by surprise because he remembered seeing them together which he described to the court, "they always had been arm-in-arm, happy." Brad said he asked Douglas if they were having marital problems, but "he said no, it was just money. He said he didn't want her to suffer. He just wanted it to be quick. He said he didn't want her abused."[10] Brad said he was angry at Glen for thinking he would consider being involved in a murder for hire plot. He immediately told Douglas he was not interested.

Deputy District Attorney Brown asked Brad if he had ever been ripped off in the amount of $40,000, alluding to the defense attorney's opening statements. Brad quickly replied, "I've never seen that much money." The next question was if Douglas had ever stolen from him. Brad did not hesitate before saying, "No, he didn't know me well enough to approach me on that type of stuff … As far as I know, he was a pretty straight guy. I never even saw him drink."[11] Douglas' attorney asked Brad why there would be "street talk" that he had been ripped off. Brad simply said, "I don't understand anything you're saying, Mr. Burt."

Glen Miller's neighbor, Dale McEwen, took the witness stand. He recalled Douglas and Glen being at his house when the topic of a drug rip-off came up. He said Douglas had left the room when the accusation that he had ripped off the Nevell brothers. Dale said he asked what was going to happen and Glen "insinuated they were after Doug." Dale told the court that weeks before Shelly was killed, Douglas and Glen were at his house when the subject of a hitman came up. He said they had all been smoking marijuana and he could not recall the exact details but he knew that no one had solicited him to kill Shelly.

Tim Brown took the witness stand and told the court that he had been friends with Jeffrey since middle school. He admitted to knowing that Jeffrey did drugs, but explained that since Jeffrey had returned from California, he had only seen him do drugs twice. Tim told the jury about a day that Jeffrey asked him to drive past the Meier and Frank store. When Tim asked why, he said Jeffrey said he could not tell him. Tim said he pressed for an answer and "Then he got mad and let it slip that 'Miller wants me to waste somebody.'" Tim said he had a hard time comprehending this because Jeffrey was not a violent person. In fact, he said, "Jeff was such a nice, pleasant guy." Tim said they did drive past the Meier and Frank store. He said later that day he overheard Jeffrey on the phone with someone saying, "I looked and I didn't see it … oh, light blue, I thought it was gray." Tim said he came forward with the information after learning that Shelly worked at Meier and Frank, that she had been murdered in a light blue car, and that her husband's last name was Miller.

The courtroom was packed the day Jeffrey took the witness stand. Jeffrey was asked how long he had known the defendant. He said he was staying at his grandparent's house when he first returned to Salem after living in California. It was there that he met Douglas. He said his uncle, Howard, introduced them. Jeffrey told the court that prior to Douglas arriving, his uncle had asked him, "if I would snuff somebody for $5,000?" He said his uncle seemed serious and, "I acted like a big shot and said, yeah, I'd do it."

Jeffrey said that days later, his uncle told him that a plan had been put into place. "It had been set up that when she got off work, she would be going by a place next to Suspenders Pizza. I was supposed to hide and get her." Jeffrey told the court that he did not take the plan seriously, and went to a party that night. He said his uncle contacted him the following day. "He wanted to know what happened. I told him it was a stupid plan, and it wouldn't work. The place wasn't set up right for it."[12]

Jeffrey testified that a few days later, he went to Douglas' house. He described the meeting with Douglas saying, "He just got right down to business, showing me a hand-drawn map of the Meier and Frank store." He described in detail the plan:

> We thought strangulation would be the way to do it. He didn't want me to touch her sexually. He wanted it to be quick. I was supposed to go down and unlock the car with the key he gave me, take it back to him, and then go down and wait in the car. He told me that he would pay me personally $5,000.[13]

Jeffrey continued his testimony, confirming that he did go to the Meier and Frank parking lot that night. He unlocked the driver's side because Douglas had told him the passenger side door was difficult to unlock. He described how he unlocked the passenger door from inside, leaving it unlocked, and went back to Douglas' house to return the key. When he left Douglas' house, he just kept going and never returned to the Meier and Frank parking lot. The next day, he told Douglas that there were too many people around.

As Jeffrey testified to a rapt audience, it appeared that Douglas was getting teary eyed. Judge Brown excused the jurors for a brief recess. He then spoke directly to Douglas saying, "The court realizes this is really an emotion-packed situation, but will ask you to watch yourself." The jurors returned to the courtroom but were told that they were being given the afternoon off so they could rest.

When court resumed, Jeffrey continued his testimony. He said that Douglas was still anxious to have the hit completed. They once again tried the parking lot scenario, but this time, Shelly got into her car and drove off. Jeffrey said he called Douglas from a payphone and explained that there were too many people around. Jeffrey said at that time, Douglas told him he would get in touch with him soon.

Jeffrey said the next time he saw Douglas was when they met outside of a bar in Salem. Douglas was preoccupied with the thought that someone other than Jeffrey and his uncle knew about his plan. Jeffrey explained, "He was worried that somebody named Nevell had recorded a conversation they had. He was worried they might try to blackmail him after it happened. He wanted to know if I would help him out if they did ... take care of them. I said, yes."[14]

Jeffrey had everyone's attention as he described the next attempt on Shelly's life. He explained that Douglas had decided against the parking lot of the Meier and Frank store due to the number of potential witnesses. Jeffrey explained, "He had it set up for her to take their son over to his sister's house. He wanted me to try it there." Jeffrey said that Douglas showed him where his sister lived but before anything could happen, he called and cancelled. As he continued his testimony, he admitted that when Douglas introduced him to Glen Miller, he used the alias of Bob Allenby. Jeffrey said, "I was really leery about people knowing who I was."

The courtroom was still as Jeffrey described the day that he murdered Shelly. He began by saying Douglas had come to his house earlier in the day. Douglas told Jeffrey that he had a plan for that night. Jeffrey told the court, "He was going to call her and have her drop off a bill or something at a credit place next to Suspenders Pizza. He said he would tell her there was going to be somebody there late."

Although Jeffrey had been resistant to using a gun in the commission of this crime, Douglas convinced him that a gun would be the best method, saying, "but he thought it was a good idea because it was quick."

Jeffrey described the rest of the day saying that in the afternoon he and Douglas went with Jeffrey's grandfather to a Fred Meyer store. That evening, he went to Douglas' house. It was then, that Douglas told him, if the murder took place that night, he would pay him $10,000. Jeffrey said he left Douglas' house and went to an arcade. He told the jury that at about 8:30 p.m., he drove to the Oregon Acceptance Company and parked his truck nearby.

You could hear a pin drop in the courtroom as Jeffrey described what happened next. He said, "I laid on my back next to the building in the bushes. Shelly Miller drove up about 10 minutes later and got out of her car. She said, 'Okay, just don't hurt me.'"[15] Jeffrey described the next moments went by in a blur.

Every person in the courtroom sat with rapt attention when Douglas' interview with Detective Vern Meighen was played. The interview had taken place two days after Shelly's body had been located. Douglas was asked by Detective Meighen to recall his activities the day his wife was killed. Douglas described a routine day, saying he left the house to get some food in the morning because Shelly was not feeling well. When he returned home, he made breakfast for her. When Shelly went back to bed about 1 p.m., he left the house and went to visit Glen Miller and "went someplace else, but I can't recall." He then returned home.

Douglas told Detective Meighen that Shelly left for work just after 4:30 p.m. He recalled his brother-in-law, Ray DeLassio, stopped by around 7:30 p.m. and stayed for an hour. Douglas said he called his wife at work to see how she was doing and then made two or three other phone calls before Glen came over at 8:55 p.m. Douglas told Detective Meighen about Jerry coming to the house and helping him look for his wife. He then told the detective how they found her car the next morning.

Douglas stressed that their marriage was fine, that they had no more problems than the average couple. When Detective Meighen asked why they were in marriage counseling, Douglas said his problem was "understanding the sensitivity of Shelly and showing her I appreciate her. If the slightest thing went wrong, she wanted assurance." Douglas did admit that he had a temper and had not always demonstrated that he appreciated her. He said he had just learned from a friend two days before her death that Shelly "worshipped our marriage until the dying end."

Douglas went on to say that Shelly had spoken to their marriage counselor, William Davis, days before and he had said, "'I can tell, Shelly, that you value your marriage a high degree and that things can work out' or something like that."

Detective Meighen told Douglas the police found a note written by Shelly that was written, "as that of a depressed person. One of the reasons we haven't talked to you about the note is that no gun was found in her car."

Douglas told Detective Meighen that he could not comprehend that his wife committed suicide. He reiterated that, "When she left Monday, she was in a great state of spirits even though she had a cold."

Detective Meighen replied, "She'd had it. She was on her way. Basically, that letter was a farewell to you." Again, Douglas said that simply could not be true.

Detective Meighen suggested to Douglas that perhaps he was trying to cover up his wife's suicide. Douglas firmly stated, "I swear to God that I never picked up a gun [from the car] and nobody I know picked up a gun."

Detective Meighen explained to the jury that prior to learning that this was a murder for hire, the police originally thought it might be a suicide. He said the police have to look at different possibilities anytime they investigate a death. He went on to say that "The only obstacle to that theory was that no gun was found in the car."

The prosecution pointed out that as Douglas described his day to Detective Meighen, he never mentioned meeting with Jeffrey. Yet Jeffrey told the investigators that he met with Douglas twice on the day Shelly died. Jeffrey's grandfather and aunt both testified that they saw the two together that day. Witnesses took the stand and stated that Douglas and Jeffrey were acquainted. This was in an effort to dispel Douglas' claim that he had only met Jeffrey once or twice when he was trying to locate Jeffrey's uncle.

The courtroom was filled to the brim the day Douglas strode to the witness stand. His first attack was on how seldom he had had any contact with Jeffrey. He stated, "If I had to get a hold of Howard Allen, Jeff Allen was the way I was supposed to go." He admitted to having had five contacts with Jeffrey in the past, but he explained them away saying he was trying to reach Jeffrey's uncle. He explained that he and Howard conducted horse racing bets together. It was Douglas' contention that Howard owed him $14,000 and that was the only reason he ever had contact with Jeffrey.

Douglas told the court he met Jeffrey when he went to the Allen family's second-hand store. Douglas was there to speak to Howard about collecting a debt Howard owed him. Douglas also admitted he had called Jeffrey in the past on four different occasions but it was always in an attempt to speak to Howard.

The jury listened as Douglas described an encounter that he had with Jeffrey three weeks before Shelly was killed. Douglas said Jeffrey showed up at his house and asked if Douglas knew where he could purchase some marijuana. Douglas admitted he gave Jeffrey some of his own marijuana with the agreement that Jeffrey would contact Howard. It was Douglas' testimony that the following day, Jeffrey called him and wanted to buy some marijuana. He said Jeffrey drove to his house and he met him outside where Jeffrey paid him $30 for the marijuana.

Although Douglas never mentioned to the police that he was in contact with Jeffrey on the day his wife was murdered, he told the jury about that encounter. He began by saying Jeffrey called him in the morning and said, "He had gotten ahold of his uncle and he had some information in regards to the money he owed me." Douglas said he drove to Jeffrey's house and asked, "What about my money?" However, "he said he didn't know." Douglas said this upset him because he had driven over to Jeffrey's house expecting an explanation. Jeffrey told him Howard would be arriving in Salem in the coming days.

Douglas recalled, "At that point Jeffrey's aunt entered the room and wanted Allen to go to the store and get her some candy. Jeff wanted me to take him." Douglas said he drove Jeffrey to a nearby Circle K store. When they returned from the Circle K store, Jeffrey's grandfather asked Douglas to take him to a Fred Meyer store and Douglas agreed to the request. He said he and Jeffrey stayed in the car while Jeffrey's grandfather went into the store.

It was then, Douglas said, that Jeffrey began acting strangely. He told the court, "I seen what was commonly known as a narcotic withdrawal." He said he recognized the symptoms from his time in the U.S. Army when he was assigned to the military police. Douglas said he saw needle marks on Jeffrey's right arm, leading him to believe Jeffrey had injected narcotics recently.

Douglas recalled Jeffrey asking who was watching D.J.? When Douglas replied that Shelly was at home with the baby, Jeffrey asked why she was not at work. Douglas said, "I don't know how he knew about her work." He remembered Jeffrey asking, "How she kept in shape. I told him she belongs to the health spa."

Douglas said later that day, soon after Shelly went to work, Jeffrey stopped by his house. After seeing him hit the curb and a shrub, Douglas refused to let him into his house. He told the jury, "He came out of the truck in an erratic manner. I wouldn't let him in my house. I had the screen door on."

The prosecution wanted to know why Douglas never mentioned these encounters to the police, and in fact, had denied having any contact with Jeffrey on the day Shelly was murdered. Deputy District Attorney Brown asked Douglas, "You mean you forgot to tell them you saw the same bizarre young man twice in the same day your wife was killed?" Douglas simply said, "I didn't think it was important at the time. I don't recall."[16]

The defense asked Douglas about his relationship with Glen Miller. Douglas answered, "I considered him a good friend but honestly someone I could not trust." He went on to say that Glen had been mixed up in drugs for months. Douglas added that the Nevell brothers had the reputation of being "gangsters."

Douglas admitted he heard people saying, "That I had stolen drugs from Brad and Lance Nevell. I told Glen I've got to talk to these people and set it straight." Glen arranged for Douglas and Brad to meet. Douglas recalled that upon seeing Brad, he said, "I came right out and said, Brad, I didn't steal nothing from you." Douglas told the court that Brad simply said, "If that's what you say, then that's okay." Douglas informed the court that a fellow inmate of his had told him that Brad had put out a contract on his life.

When his attorney asked him why he thought Shelly had been murdered, he simply said, "the so-called talk that I was ripping off the drugs." He expanded on that thought and said, "I loved her. I put her on a pedestal, even higher than myself. We didn't have the marriage problems like a lot of people." He added that they did not have "financial problems, infidelity, brutality or drinking," like other couples did. He conceded their only problem was, "I couldn't show her the affection to the degree that she needed. I didn't share the responsibilities with her. I kept things from her. I honestly believe in my heart, as I'm sitting here now, that the marriage would have worked."[17] Douglas denied ever having an affair with Carol. Douglas was on the witness stand for more than three hours. When he stepped down, the attorneys began their closing statements.

Deputy District Attorney Brown described Douglas as a "cold and calculating person." He added, "He's not without emotion because he did not hate Shelly Miller. He probably didn't even dislike her. The fact of the matter is she just got expendable." He told the jurors that the Miller's marriage, "went far beyond the garden-variety of marital problems. There was a profound change in her attitude. She could not carry on the struggle any longer of keeping her marriage going." He reminded the jury the only source of income for the couple, was Shelly's part time job at Meier and Frank. Their life insurance policies went into effect weeks before Shelly was killed. Deputy District Attorney Brown said Douglas wanted to ensure their son's future, if both he and Shelly died. Referring to Douglas' daughter from his first marriage, he told the jury, "There was no history of making financial arrangements to secure the future of his first child."[18]

Deputy District Attorney Brown pointed out that Douglas never told the police that he knew Jeffrey, let alone that he had two encounters with Jeffrey on the day Shelly was killed. He told the jury, "He was keeping some distance between him and Jeff Allen." He added that Douglas tried "to hide the fact that he knew Jeff Allen—the one person in Marion County he did not want police talking to."[19]

Deputy District Attorney Brown told the panel of jurors, "Doug Miller is as responsible for Shelly Miller's death as Jeff Allen is and he ought to be held accountable." In referring to Jeffrey's plea bargain agreement, he said:

> It is the process where you look for the truth and allocate responsibility. Some people would prefer that Allen never be released from prison, but in reality, you do not always

> get what you want. You have to make decisions about what you want to give up to hold others accountable.[20]

Douglas' defense attorney, Charles told the jurors that Douglas could not possibly be guilty of the accusations against him. He asked the jurors:

> If they could conceive of a man so cold that he would order a birthday cake for his wife and kiss her goodbye as she leaves for work, knowing full well that he was going to kill her before the birthday party ... That doesn't even happen in *The Godfather*. That's too much.[21]

In referring to the prosecution's stance that Douglas asked multiple people to recommend a hitman, Charles told the jury Douglas "was too smart to go grocery shopping for someone to kill his wife."

Charles said he had "never seen a case of more unmitigated perjurers." He asked, "How many lies can you have in a case where they want you to convict a man for aggravated murder?"

The defense had maintained all along that Shelly was killed due to her husband's drug activity but that he had nothing to do with the actual murder. Charles told the jury, "There is within this community a separate and distinct culture—a drug culture. That culture affected Douglas and Shelly Miller. They killed his wife and now they'd like to have you put him away for them."

Charles told the jury that the District Attorney's Office accepted a plea agreement with Jeffrey that was an "an abuse of the system. If this system comes to the point where some punk can bargain away a thirty-year mandatory sentence, then the system is done."

When both sides finished their closing statements, the trial came to a close after almost two weeks. The case was given to the jury to begin their deliberations. Four hours later, the jury announced that they had reached a unanimous verdict. Douglas stood emotionless with his hands folded and as the words, guilty of aggravated murder were read. Sentencing was scheduled at a later date.

Prior to Douglas' trial, Shelly's sister, Shawnee, had petitioned the court for legal guardianship of D.J. She and her husband had taken care of the infant immediately following Shelly's death. They turned the baby over to Douglas before he was arrested. At the time, he was staying with his parents. The baby remained with Douglas' parents after his arrest. Polk County Circuit Judge Darrell Williams awarded custody to Shawnee but granted a stay to Douglas' parents who said they would appeal. Judge Williams said he awarded Shawnee custody because she and her husband were young and they had a toddler.

A private investigator who had worked for Charles reported that his office had been entered one evening and three cassette tapes pertaining to the murder had been stolen. The cassette tapes had been in a locked filing cabinet. The cassette tapes were missing, but in their place was a bag of marijuana. The police did not find any signs of forced entry.

Douglas' defense counsel requested a new trial based on new evidence. He also claimed the prosecution had withheld evidence about Brad Nevell. At a hearing in front of Judge Clarke Brown, Charles brought forth three witnesses who were supposed to claim that it was actually Brad who killed Shelly. Everything fell apart when one of the witnesses retracted what he had stated in his affidavit.

An inmate of Douglas' came forward with information. He said Douglas offered to sign over his 1981 Datsun pickup valued at $5,000 in exchange for helping him secure a new trial. A promise was allegedly made for additional funds if Douglas was acquitted at his new trial and received the life insurance money. The inmate told Judge Brown he was retracting his statement after realizing he could receive additional time on his sentence for perjury. He also feared for his safety and the safety of his finance. Douglas told Judge Brown, "I didn't promise nothing. When I heard he had written a statement, I didn't even know him."

Charles also argued that the prosecution made arrangements to dismiss five charges against Brad in exchange for his testimony. Judge Brown stated there was "nothing to show me Mr. Nevell is being treated other than any other type of individual."

Charles contended the prosecution violated discovery laws by failing to inform him that Brad had been convicted of burglary years before. Judge Brown told Charles, "Since Nevell had admitted on the stand that he was a drug dealer, knowing that he had been convicted of burglary several years ago would not have influenced the jury's perception of his credibility."

Judge Brown ruled in favor of the prosecution's request for Douglas to reimburse the state $2,926 for costs incurred. District Attorney Scruggs asked that liens be attached to Douglas' vehicles to cover the costs. Judge Brown denied the motion for a new trial. He sentenced Douglas to life in prison with a minimum of thirty years before being eligible for parole, work release, temporary leave, or employment at a forest camp or a work camp.

After Jeffrey finished testifying at Douglas' trial, he appeared before Judge Barber for sentencing. District Attorney Scruggs told Judge Barber that Shelly "would be dead regardless of Jeff Allen's actions. If Jeff Allen had not killed her, someone else would have. It was imperative that we hold Doug Miller responsible. Without Allen's cooperation, that might not have been possible." Judge Barber noted that although Jeffrey had remorse for what he had done, the act was premediated, calculated, and cold-blooded. He told Jeffrey, "You deprived a child of its mother, parents of a daughter, and you deprived a woman of a long, fruitful life. You should be punished for what you've done."[22] Judge Barber sentenced Jeffrey to life in prison with a minimum of five years for committing the crime with a gun. Judge Barber recommended he serve ten years before being eligible for parole.

The next trial was Howard Allen's. He was facing a charge of aggravated murder. Howard appeared before Judge Duane Ertsgaard and pled no contest to a charge of solicitation to commit murder. His attorney, Paul Ferder, told reporters that his client did not want to risk a roll of the dice that could have resulted in a sentence of life in prison with a minimum of thirty years. Howard was now looking at a sentence of twenty years. Paul was confident the sentence would be much less due to Howard's lack of a criminal history.

Details emerged about Howard's involvement with the murder for hire plot. He told investigators that the plan had been put in place weeks before it occurred. He said at one time Douglas also wanted his mother-in-law killed as well as his infant son. Howard allegedly asked Douglas, "'Are you thinking about a package deal?' He said Douglas just laughed." The prosecution stated that both Howard and Jeffrey were to receive $10,000. Judge Ertsgaard accepted the plea of solicitation to commit murder. Howard was sentenced to eighteen years in prison, with a minimum of six years served before being eligible for parole.

On the day that Shelly would have turned twenty-four, her family had a letter to the editor published in the *Statesman Journal*. The letter read:

> To the Editor: Today, February 23, marks Shelly Terwilliger Miller's 24th birthday. It was also a year ago, February 22, 1982 that Shelly was murdered. Her murderers have been convicted and are currently serving sentences.
>
> The custody of her son, D.J. was decided in August 1982. Shelly's sister and brother-in-law were awarded custody, but he remains at the home of Mr. and Mrs. E. Miller, the paternal grandparents. A court date of March 30 has been set at the Court of Appeals to hopefully resolve this matter.
>
> We the Terwilliger family wish to express our gratitude and deeply felt appreciation to Shelly's many friends for their sympathy and support during the past year. We also wish to express our appreciation to those we were in closest contact with in the district attorney's office and in the Salem Police Department for their outstanding work and sensitivity in handling this case. The Terwilliger Family. Salem, Oregon.[23]

The Oregon Court of Appeals awarded D.J. to Shawnee and her husband, Roger. D.J. was eighteen months old at the time.

Jeffrey was back in the news after he made a break for freedom in 1984. Jeffrey was serving time at the Oregon State Correctional Institution. The prison was undergoing a $300,000 security renovation. One aspect of that renovation was to remove the coiled razor wire fencing. When part of the fence was down, Jeffrey and a fellow inmate saw the opportunity for freedom. A prison guard in one of the towers initially thought they were part of the work crew. When he realized they were in fact, inmates, he hollered at them to stop. When they kept going, he fired three warnings shots, before starting to fire at them using a long-range rifle. The pair of escapees managed to get over two fences and avoid more than thirty rounds fired at them before being captured in a nearby apple orchard.

Oregon State Correctional Institution Superintendent George Sullivan said they were lucky to be alive. He said the new system would eliminate the need for guards to be in the towers and instead would have a state-of-the-art television and audio monitoring system. He explained that prison guards would patrol the fence line in four-wheel-drive vehicles. George told the *Statesman Journal*, "These two men are rather typical of our inmate population. They are young, healthy and strong and serving a lot of time for very serious crimes." The two escapees were treated for cuts at the Oregon State Correctional Institution's hospital and then placed in maximum security. Jeffrey received another eighteen months for his escape attempt.

In 1983, attorney John Hingson represented Douglas in his appeal. The Oregon Court of Appeals affirmed his conviction without opinion. The following year, his post-conviction relief petition was denied by Clackamas County Circuit Judge Charles Sams.

In October 1990, Douglas filed a lawsuit against his defense attorney, Charles Burt and his post-conviction appeal attorney John Hingson. In the lawsuit, he asked for $9.5 million from Charles and $3 million from John. He also filed a new post-conviction appeal.

Douglas claimed that Charles did not call a key witness in his original trial and his failure to do so was negligent. Douglas believed there was an eye witness to the murder. The eye witness allegedly was near the crime when it happened and saw a "large blondish-haired man" walk away from Shelly's car immediately after hearing a gunshot. The man walked to a Chevy Luv pickup truck where another man was waiting for him. According to Douglas, the following morning the witness returned to the scene of the crime and this time was threatened by the "large blondish-haired man." Douglas said that the witness gave the name of the man to the police but Charles never followed through with the eye witness. In the lawsuit, Douglas claimed that John failed to bring up the eye witness account and also failed to state that Charles had been negligent.

Circuit Court Judge Thomas Mosgrove ruled that Douglas had missed the opportunity to file the lawsuit within the two-year statute of limitations. Douglas argued that he lacked the information that he needed until 1990, so therefore the clock should not have begun ticking until that time. Judge Mosgrove informed Douglas that if the issues he claimed were true at that time, they were equally true ten years before. Judge Mosgrove dismissed the lawsuit and the request for a new trial. Two years later, the Oregon Court of Appeals affirmed Judge Mosgrove's decision.

In 1992, Shelly's mother, Joan Terwilliger, wrote a letter that was published in the *Statesman Journal*. The letter read:

> I wish to inform anyone interested that Douglas Miller convicted of aggravated murder August 5, 1982 of Shelly [Terwilliger] Miller, age 22, and sentenced to life with a 30-year mandatory minimum sentence, after exhausting all appeals has submitted an application for executive clemency to Governor Barbara Roberts to rescind the minimum sentence. Please express your opinion by writing immediately to Governor Roberts. Thank you for your support in the past.[24]

4

Leroy Darnall

While the community of Drain was celebrating America's bicentennial over the Fourth of July weekend, the town pharmacist, Leroy Darnall, was murdered. His body was found in the loft of the pharmacy on July 6, 1976, by an employee who arrived for work.

When the police arrived, they immediately noticed the safe was wide open, however it did not appear that any money was missing from the safe. There were numerous drugs strewn around, but the police did not believe any drugs were missing. The autopsy revealed Leroy, age fifty-one, was the victim of a homicide, having been bludgeoned to death. The investigators were unable to locate the murder weapon.

A seven-state alert was issued for Leroy's car. The detectives believed the car had been used as a getaway vehicle. Leroy's family offered a $2,500 reward for the return of the car, hoping that would lead to the person who had murdered Leroy. Two months after the murder, an off-duty police officer, Raymond Tercek, located the car at a parking lot in Portland. The investigators believed it had been abandoned in the parking lot. Officer Tercek was not eligible for the reward money due to his official capacity.

Douglas County District Attorney Bill Lasswell, along with Douglas County Sheriff Merle Jensen and Oregon State Police Lieutenant Marion Hardy, held a press conference a year after the murder. They announced that Leroy's son, Nathan, age twenty-two, and his friend David Wright, age twenty-three, had been arrested in Decatur, Georgia, for the murder of Leroy Darnall. They told the reporters the crime had been a murder for hire contract. They alleged that Nathan hired David to murder his father. At the press conference it was announced that a deputy sheriff and two state troopers were leaving for Georgia to interview both Nathan and David. In the meantime, the district attorney's office was beginning the extradition process.

Neither Nathan nor David fought extradition to Oregon. They were brought to Roseburg and lodged at the Douglas County Jail. At the time of David's arrest, he was married and had an infant son. David pled innocent to the charge of murder. Days before David was to go on trial, he pled guilty to killing Leroy Darnall. David was sentenced to life in prison. In his confession, he said he beat Leroy to death because he loved him as a father and could not bear the thought of someone else shooting him.

Nathan pled innocent by reason of mental illness or defect. Nathan's trial was postponed for several months at the request of both the prosecution and the defense. The trial got underway three years after the murder. Judge Don Sanders presided over the trial. Deputy District Attorney Charles Lee represented the prosecution and defense attorney, Gary Hill, represented Nathan. The jury was made up of eight women and four men.

In Deputy District Attorney Lee's opening statement, he said Nathan arranged for the murder of his father, out of pure greed. He explained that Nathan would receive not only the life insurance proceeds, but would also benefit from the family's estate.

Gary's opening statements painted an entirely different picture—one where Nathan was forced by his father to hire a hitman because his father did not want to commit suicide. Gary explained that Leroy was heavily in debt to local drug dealers.

David testified against Nathan during his trial. He told the jury that Leroy was like a father to him, and they referred to one another as "Dad" and "Son." David said he considered himself a part of the Darnall family. David said Nathan had solicited him to kill his father and offered him a portion of Leroy's estate if he would commit the murder. David said he was told his portion could be as high as $20,000. David told the court that Leroy was in trouble with people in the illegal drug business. He said Leroy had threatened suicide in the past, but also his life had been threatened by drug associates. David said Nathan was concerned about his father. David would not answer any questions from either side regarding details of the murder.

Nathan's defense attorney, Gary Hill, told the court Leroy orchestrated the murder through his son in an effort to be done with the drug dealers he was involved with and owed $50,000 to. Gary also told the court that Nathan suffered from a mental disorder that he described as "alternating multiple personality." Two psychiatrists and a clinical psychologist testified that Nathan did have a multiple personality disorder that prevented him from conforming to the law.

Dr. Bennett Braun of Chicago was one of the psychiatrists who testified. He told the jury that Nathan suffered from three personalities. He listed them as: Nathan, Ned, and Nate. Dr. Braun said Nathan was an alert, self-confident, scowling, and sometimes hostile personality. Ned, on the other hand, was a weak, cowering, easily influenced person. Nate was affable, smiling, and approachable. He told the court that he saw all three personalities after extensive interviews and psychological tests. He said the three distinct personalities differed in facial expressions, muscle tone, attitude, voice characteristics, and even handwriting. Dr. Braun explained Nathan's troubled family history was a key factor in his developing multiple personalities.

It was Dr. Braun's opinion, that Ned was pressured by his father to hire a hitman. He told the court "Ned was unable to resist the urging of his father, with whom he shared an abnormal dependence." According to Dr. Braun, it was Ned who hired David to be the hitman. Dr. Paul Basford of Springfield, Oregon, testified that as a trained psychiatrist, he believed Nathan had at least two different personalities.

When Nathan took the witness stand, he switched between two personalities. Those in the courtroom may have noticed Ned answered questions for the first hour. He was visibly shaking, cowering, stuttering, and having difficulties speaking. But then Nathan took over and was strong and confident.

Nathan explained to the jury that he and his father referred to his other personality as Ned. He added that Nathan knew about Ned, but Ned was not aware of any other personalities. He said it was Nathan's job to protect Ned anytime he became upset or scared.

Nathan told the court while he was living in Atlanta, Georgia prior to his father's death, he received a phone call from his father. During the phone call, his father told him he owed $50,000 to drug dealers from the illegal drug business he had gotten himself wrapped up in. Nathan said his mother had died a few years prior and she incurred a great deal of medical expenses, all of which his father paid. Nathan added that debt collectors had called him in Atlanta looking for his father. He said his father asked him to pay his creditors using the proceeds from his life insurance.

The prosecution argued that Nathan hired David to kill his father so that he could receive Leroy's life insurance fund. They called psychiatrist, Dr. Stanley Abrams, to the stand. He stated he did not think multiple personalities was a sufficient mental defect to justify being acquitted of murder. He further stated that it was possible that Nathan was faking the multiple personalities.

The defense called witnesses who testified that Leroy was heavily in debt. They spoke of his involvement with an illegal drug ring that he was supplying drugs to. Nathan's wife, and his brother, both told the court they had received threats from an unknown source in the weeks leading up to Nathan's trial. The wife of Nathan's former court appointed attorney, Ron Poole, told the court she had received two phone calls saying if, "Ned" talks, her husband would be killed.

The jury got the case on a Thursday evening and they deliberated until 2 a.m. Friday morning. The jury found Nathan guilty of murder. Nathan was sentenced to life in prison. Nathan put his time to good use in prison. He requested permission to be allowed to work in the vocational electronics training field. That field was generally not open to people serving life terms. The field was intended for inmates to learn a skill prior to being released from prison.

Once Nathan was allowed into the vocational area, he invented what he named "The Silent Signal." It was a device worn by hearing impaired people to alert them to certain sounds. The device consisted of a small portable transmitter that was secured on a belt worn by the person. There was a button on the device that could be pushed to receive a vibration when a sound such as a telephone or a doorbell rang as long as the other part was attached to that device. The attachment could also be secured to a door or window so the person would know if either had been opened.

Nathan told reporters that he did not have hearing capability in one ear, and had only partial hearing in the other ear. Nathan said in high school he was diagnosed with hearing loss but he chose not to wear hearing aids for fear of being bullied by his classmates. He said as a child, he would ignore people, rather than asking them to speak up. He said he alleviated his loneliness by tinkering with machines. It was not until he was incarcerated that he began wearing hearing aids. He told a reporter from the *Roseburg News-Review*, "For the first time in my life, I could hear a conversation more than thirty feet away. And what a lot of noise there was."

A fifteen-year-old boy was the first recipient of "The Silent Signal." The boy's father provided Nathan with the materials he needed. Nathan also worked with the Hillsboro School District to provide hearing impaired students with the device so they would know if a fire alarm sounded, or if the school bell rang. He incorporated different lights on the device that corresponded to the different bells they would hear at school.

Nathan's next invention was to modify a Mowat sensor for a wheelchair-bound sixteen-year-old girl in Portland. By modifying the sensor to her needs, she was better able to locate objects. In addition to working on electronic inventions, Nathan took college classes and completed three Associate of Science degrees in: Management, Computer Programming-Microcomputer, and Computer Electronics Technology from Chemeketa Community College. As Nathan progressed with his inventions, he wrote a letter that was published in the *Statesman Journal*. The letter read:

> To the Oregon Statesman:
>
> I am presently incarcerated at the Oregon State Penitentiary. During a visit with my grandmother, it was suggested that I might write you for help.
>
> I have a couple of inventions or ideas that just might be useful and practical, but since I am in prison, I cannot pursue any of them. I don't have the money for a patent attorney, or the money and help to build working models.
>
> I have heard of attorneys and people that get involved in these types of things and take their pay out of the profits that are made off the invention.
>
> I would appreciate any help that you could give me.
>
> Nathan E. Darnall
>
> Salem, Oregon[1]

In 1982, Mitch Lipka of the *Statesman Journal* interviewed Nathan about his inventions. Nathan gave more background information about his family. He told Mitch that he and his brother shared a house with his adopted brother, his adopted sister, and his parents. He said his father was an alcoholic who was unable to cope with the pressures of life. His mother had polio and ended up in a nursing home. He told the reporter, "I had this real strong fear of being different."

Nathan recalled spending hours alone in the family's basement tinkering with electronics. He recalled, "If I could take it apart and look into it, I'd do it. I graduated into cars. I understood how the car worked so well, I could almost understand what the car was going through."

He told Mitch of one memory that continued to haunt him. He was in Eugene scheduled to race a car. He wanted to go to the nursing home to visit his mother, but he feared he would miss his starting time. He chose to go to the race instead of visiting his mother. His mother died that night. Nathan told Mitch, "After that, things just started falling apart."

Nathan told Mitch that once he was incarcerated, he had to rethink his life. He said, "I'm sitting inside the penitentiary saying … what happened?" He then decided, "I've got a choice. I can waste time or I can focus on to something that will help people. I am learning more about myself every day, soul searching. I can honestly say I have found God."[2]

When talking to Mitch about his inventions, he said, "I want to do something productive. There are people who are walking around in circles and don't know what they are doing … I don't want to do that."[3]

A prison official, Charles Keaton told Mitch, "He had an idea. He carried it through. He's unique in that way. In the twenty-three years I've been in this business, this is the only time I've seen anybody go with it."[4]

Also, in 1982, a reporter for the *Albany Democrat-Herald*, asked Nathan what his plans were for when he was released? He figured he "can do about seventeen more projects—one every six months—before his release date in 1990." When asked what type of work he wanted to do in the future, he replied, "You know, I've really done a lot of soul-searching and thinking about that. I would really like to teach the handicapped or work with them. I'd really enjoy that."[5]

Nathan continued working on electronic inventions. He invented a device to be used by autistic children that helped adults know if the child was understanding what was being said. He also invented a device that allowed paralyzed people to be able to turn on a television or dial a telephone with the blink of an eye. In 1985, he came up with a way for a blind person to use a computer.

Nathan had to rely on organizations and individuals to donate materials so that he could continue his work. He and his wife set up a non-profit, Handicap Systems Research, that distributed his inventions. Nathan told the *Albany Democrat-Herald*:

> If these were designed on the street, they'd really be expensive because you're paying for a lot of engineering time. The thing we have here is time. My biggest restriction is that most handicapped people don't have money, and we don't have money. The nice thing about this is, since we're already locked up, it allows us to be productive at the same time. It allows us to be people, not just numbers. That's a good feeling.[6]

Nathan's wife and son visited him on a regular basis but towards the end of his prison sentence, they began divorce proceedings.

5
Robert Firth

In September 1976, deputies from the Washington County Sheriff's Office were dispatched to a homicide at a 7-11 store in Aloha. Three customers had entered the store and found the body of the store owner in the walk-in cooler. The deputies identified the store owner as Robert Firth, age forty-seven. He had been shot in the head four times. Initially, it appeared to be a random holdup of the 7-11 store.

When the deputies arrived, they immediately noticed the cash register tills were empty. One deputy recalled having just been at the store ten minutes prior and speaking to Robert. The store manager, Tom Sanders, told the investigators that early in the morning when Robert was shot, there was generally not much cash in the till.

Within days, Robert's wife, Donna, age thirty-four, Kerry McKendall, age twenty-seven, of Hillsboro, Bette Carter, age forty-four, of Aloha, and Michael Umscheid, age twenty-one, of Hillsboro were arrested. All four were booked into the Washington County jail.

When it came time for Deputy District Attorney Robert Wasson to explain to Washington County Circuit Judge Harold Lewis why the three women had been arrested, he was ill prepared to do so. The three women were released from jail. Hours later, the Washington County grand jury handed down indictments for all three women. The women were located and rearrested. Desmond Connall, the attorney representing Kerry, blamed the district attorney for holding the women unlawfully, and without bail, while waiting for the grand jury's decision. The prosecution said they were unable to get evidence or witnesses in time for the hearing before Judge Lewis. Days later, the Washington County grand jury indicted Roy Mattingly, age eighteen.

As it turned out, Michael should not have been free at the time of the murder. He had been released from the Oregon Correctional Institution earlier in the year after serving time for stealing a car. Two months prior to the murder, his parole had been revoked after the authorities learned he was allegedly involved in a burglary, arson, car theft, and was in possession of a weapon. The paperwork slipped through the cracks and Michael was never arrested.

Washington County District Attorney Ray Robinette, believed Michael was the actual shooter. He described the murder as an "execution." Donna's attorneys asked the court to move her trial to another county, citing the publicity the case had received. They believed she would not get a fair trial in Washington County.

Michael's trial got underway four months after the murder. He pled innocent by reason of mental disease or defect. His defense attorney explained that Michael could only be partially responsible, due to his excessive use of drugs and alcohol. District Attorney Ray Robinette began his opening statements by saying Michael was paid $1,000 by Robert's wife, Donna, to murder Robert. He explained that $500 was paid before the murder and the remaining $500 was paid after Robert was killed. District Attorney Robinette explained that Donna stood to receive $200,000–$250,000 from her husband's life insurance proceeds. District Attorney Robinette told the court Roy Mattingly would testify that Michael asked for his help in carrying out the murder.

Washington County Deputy Medical Examiner, Eugene Jacobus, told the jury Robert had been shot in the head four times with a .22 caliber weapon. Many witnesses took the stand including the deputies who arrived on scene and the witnesses who found the body. At the end of the trial, the jury filed out to begin deliberations. It only took them ninety minutes to find Michael guilty of murder. Michael waived his right to a delay in sentencing, saying he wanted to go to prison as soon as possible. Judge Gregory Milnes sentenced Michael to life in prison. He added that he would recommend that Michael never be paroled.

Roy was charged with murder. He pled innocent by reason of mental disease or defect. He later changed his plea to guilty of first-degree manslaughter. Judge Hollie Pihl sentenced Roy to twenty years in the Oregon State Penitentiary. Both Donna and Bette agreed to testify against Kerry in exchange for a lesser sentence. They each received twenty years in prison for their role in the murder of Donna's husband.

Roy was brought from the prison to the Washington County Jail during Kerry's trial so that he could testify. Before that could happen, he made a break from freedom. He was 5 feet, 9 inches and weighed 105 pounds. He stole some grease and applied it to his body. He managed to slip through a 7-inch opening used to transport food-serving trays. Once he got through that opening, he kicked out a window on the second story. From there, he jumped to the ground, breaking two toes in the process. Within four hours, he was captured and returned to the jail.

When Kerry's trial began, the prosecution told the jury that Kerry was responsible for hiring the hitman and providing the weapon used in the commission of the crime. The jury was told that Donna was the one who asked Kerry to find a hitman to murder her husband. The jury deliberated for eleven hours before finding Kerry guilty of murder. At the time, she had four small children at home. She was sentenced to life in prison.

A year after Michael's trial, the Oregon Court of Appeals granted him a new trial. This was necessary because of a change in an Oregon Supreme Court ruling having to do with a person needing to prove they were partially responsible for their actions. Michael remained in prison awaiting the new trial. In the end, he was still found guilty of murder.

The Oregon Court of Appeals reversed Kerry's conviction and ordered that a new trial be held. They ruled that she had been illegally held as a witness before being charged with a crime. They described it as a flagrant violation of state law.

By the time the new trial began in 1979, Kerry was five months pregnant with her fifth child. Her physician testified she could have a miscarriage due to the stress of the trial. Judge Donald Ashmanskas was not swayed and the trial continued.

Soon after, Kerry accepted a plea bargain that stipulated she plea no contest to a charge of second-degree manslaughter. Deputy District Attorney Scott Upham accepted the lesser charge due to time constraints imposed by the Oregon Court of Appeals.

Twelve years into Michael's sentence, he saw a chance at freedom and took it. He had been moved from maximum security to minimum security, in anticipation of his parole in three years. As an inmate of the minimum-security section, Michael was allowed to work with the Department of Corrections Industry. In 1988, he and a fellow inmate were helping deliver office furniture at the Commerce Building in downtown Salem. The truck driver went inside the building, leaving the two inmates in the truck. Michael made a bid for freedom and took off running. The other inmate stayed in the truck. Michael was captured when police showed up at his wife's house.

The chairman of the Oregon Parole Board, Vern Faatz, told reporter Dan Postrel of the *Statesman Journal*, "Why this guy left the institution is beyond me. He had everything in the world going for him. He really screwed up. He's going to lose all this." Steve Gassner, an assistant to the Oregon State Penitentiary superintendent, explained that most inmates would not be given minimum security status so far ahead of their release date. He said Michael had proven to them that he was a good candidate through his behavior. The parole board had studied his case and noted the others involved in Robert's death had received lesser sentences. Based on that, and Michael's behavior in prison, they set his release date for 1991. Originally, he was not scheduled for a parole hearing until 2006.[1]

The Department of Corrections spokesperson, Robey Eldridge, explained that on any given day, hundreds of inmates work at various jobs:

> For a lot of these people, they've never had to get up at 7 in the morning and be somewhere at 8, and be there for four or six or eight hours and then go home, eat and go to bed. It establishes a work routine for them.[2]

Robey went on to explain that some inmates at the minimum-security section were granted trusty status, allowing them to work outside the prison walls. He said some trusties worked at the farm annex, milking cows, tending crops, and doing farm chores. Others worked in state offices answering telephones, typing documents, and doing clerical work. Others like Michael worked in the industry department. Inmates also maintained parks, forests, prison grounds, and state-owned properties. He said that although there are not guards watching them, they do have supervisors. He explained:

> Minimum security means they are trusted to be about the business of doing certain things and being there when they're supposed to be. Minimum-security inmates are not under wraps all the time. Trusty inmates are often sent out on jobs. He just violated the trust we placed in him. Each time there is an escape, we have to review all of our procedures, but we don't bring everything to a screeching halt.[3]

Michael's wife was arrested for hindering a fugitive but released soon after due to overcrowding at the jail. She received three years' probation for hindering a fugitive when she hid Michael from the authorities. Michael pled innocent to escape. He was found guilty of escape and an additional year was added to his sentence.

6
Kathryn Martini-Lissy

When the Eugene Police Department was called to the Valley River Inn on July 6, 1984, they feared they were dealing with a serial killer. Two other women had been murdered in the past month in Eugene but neither case had been solved.

In this case, the victim was Kathryn Ann Martini-Lissy, age twenty-six. She had arrived in Eugene on July 5, 1984. She rented a hotel room at the Valley River Inn for one night so she could attend a business meeting in Eugene the following day. When she failed to check out of the hotel, the hotel maid went to her room to check on her. It was at that time the employee discovered Kathryn's body.

The following day, Lieutenant Jan Clements of the Eugene Police Department told reporters her death was being investigated as a homicide because of "circumstances surrounding the crime scene and the autopsy report. We have absolutely not settled on any motives. We have potential motives." He added that they did not have any suspects.

The detectives soon learned that Kathryn was a newlywed, having just married Michael Lissy six months prior to her death. She lived in Lake Oswego and worked as a commercial loan officer for FNB Financial Company in Portland. She had recently been elected president of Portland's Network of Business and Professional Women. A friend of Kathryn's, Carole Barkley, said, "She's an absolutely super person. She's been very successful in her career. I can't believe this has happened."

The Portland-based Network of Business and Professional Women offered a reward for information leading to the arrest of the person(s) responsible for Kathyrn's murder.

The investigation led detectives to Kathryn's husband. Three months after Kathryn was murdered, the Lane County grand jury indicted Michael David Lissy, age thirty-five, and David Dean Wilson, age thirty-one, on charges of aggravated murder and conspiracy to commit a felony. The police believed Michael paid David $5,000 to murder Kathryn so he could collect on her $190,000 life insurance policy.

Michael was arrested at his parent's home in Lincoln Beach. David was arrested near his home in Beaverton. Both Michael and David pled innocent to the charges of aggravated murder and conspiracy to commit a felony. They requested court-appointed counsel. Michael's mother, Patricia Lissy, told a reporter with the Associated Press:

> The only thing we know is that he is innocent of any wrongdoing in this. The Sunday before she was murdered, they were here and she told me they decided to start their family. They were so happy. She was a wonderful, wonderful girl and he loved her very much. We all did.[1]

One thing that bothered the investigators was that there was no sign of forced entry in the hotel room where Kathryn's body was located. The investigators were able to piece together that a woman gained access to the room under false pretenses and then let David into the hotel room. The woman left the hotel room prior to the murder, but drove the getaway car back to Portland. Detectives from the Eugene Police Department arrested Gretchen Schumacher, age twenty, and charged her with aggravated murder.

Prior to Gretchen's trial, her defense attorney, John Halpern, Jr., asked Lane County Circuit Judge Edwin Allen for the state to pay $450 for a psychiatric examination for his client who he believed might suffer from a mental disease or defect. Judge Allen granted the request. While they were waiting for the psychiatric examination, Gretchen pled innocent to aggravated murder.

"A particularly degenerate individual who put money at the top of his list," were the opening remarks of District Attorney Brian Barnes at Michael's trial. He went on to say that "greed was behind this murder."[2] He explained that Michael hired David for $5,000 to murder his wife so that he could collect $190,000 from her life insurance policy.

Michael's defense attorney, Ronald Sticka told the court that although Michael frequently misrepresented himself to others, he did not want his wife murdered. He explained, "He's been an individual with an active imagination. Mr. Lissy would pass himself off to other people as something he is not."[3] Ronald expanded on the statement saying that at times Michael told people he was a graduate of Harvard University, that he was a consultant to the State Department, and that he had been an ambassador to a country in Africa.

Ronald said, in reality, Michael attended a community college, he worked at a convenience store before owning two scuba shops. One of the scuba shops went bankrupt, while the other was repossessed by the former owner when Michael could not make the payments.

Ronald told the court, "Mr. Lissy is not a monster. He got caught up in circumstances that were part of his own making." Ronald further explained that although Michael had spoken about committing a murder, he never intended to do so. Ronald said that it was David and two or three other people who murdered Kathryn and then blackmailed Michael.

The jury learned that Kathyrn attended a Catholic elementary and secondary school. When she was in the eighth grade, her classmates voted her "Best All-Around Girl." Kathyrn graduated with academic honors from the Mary Louis Academy in Queens, New York. She received multiple offers from colleges but chose to attend Yale University. She excelled at swimming and diving and was an Ivy League diver in 1978. While attending the university, she participated in the Big Sister Program, founded a woman's consciousness-raising group, was captain of a co-ed touch football team, and was a student counselor. Upon graduating, Kathyrn was accepted into the Bank of Boston's loan officer training program. She transferred to the Portland branch of their subsidiary, FBN Financial Company, three years prior to her death.

Michael's trial had barely gotten underway when a female witness took the stand. She described herself as a former prostitute. She said Michael had been a regular client of hers for the past several months. She testified Michael told her he wanted to hire a hitman. The witness told the court:

> He mentioned to me three specific hits he wanted done. One was a young woman he wanted strangled to death and possibly raped. The second was a young man he wanted beaten to within an inch of his life. And the third hit was an old couple.

The young witness told the jury Michael asked her to make two phone calls to help him find a hitman. She described that the woman he wanted killed "would think she was involved in a drug deal and he would have her in a set place."[4]

The witness said she contacted the Eugene Police Department upon learning of Kathryn's death. She said she became hysterical when she realized, "It was the same manner of death he described to me." She said she agreed to help the police by allowing them to tape record her conversations with Michael and agreed to let them record a face-to-face meeting. The young female witness told the jury that since she learned of the murder, she was no longer involved with prostitution and had enrolled in school. She said she turned down the reward money that was offered. When the prosecution asked why she decided to come forward, she replied, "Because Kathy Martini-Lissy was beautiful and successful and was doing something decent, and that's what I want to do. It's decent and it's human."[5]

In one of the tape-recorded telephone conversations, Michael allegedly told the witness that David could take responsibility for the murder, serve his sentence in prison, and then collect his payoff when he was released from prison. In another tape-recorded conversation, Michael allegedly told the witness the police did not have a case against him.

Things were going from bad to worse when the next witness took the stand. This witness also told the court she met Michael when she was working as a prostitute. She wasted no time in telling the court:

> A friend of mine told me that Michael wanted to date me, so I called him, and I met him there and I dated him and then he asked me if I could find somebody to kill somebody.

> He said he wanted a lady preferably strangled and raped or like hit over the head or something like that.

This witness admitted that she was the one who initially set up the meeting between Michael and David. She said two days before the murder took place, Michael gave David money for a new suit and a haircut. He also gave him money to rent a car to drive from his home in Beaverton to the hotel in Eugene where Kathryn was staying. The witness said she heard him tell David he needed the murder completed by 8 p.m. on Thursday, July 5. She said Michael agreed to pay David $5,000. The witness received immunity from prosecution in exchange for testifying.

The witness said she saw David about midnight on the night of the murder. She recalled David describing what happened by saying, "She let him into the room and she asked him why Michael was setting her up."

The jury then heard a tape-recorded conversation between the witness and Michael two months after the murder. In the conversation, the witness tells Michael that David is very nervous and wants more money. The witness tells Michael that David is wondering what to tell the police? Michael then says that David should turn himself in and tell the police he killed Kathyrn. Michael tells the witness that he will pay David $25,000 for taking the blame for the murder. Michael is heard to say, "I don't care what goes down, I'm saying I'm innocent. Tell him don't take any deals or there's no money."

Just when things could not get much worse for Michael, his former wife was called to the stand. She admitted Michael had offered to pay her $10,000 to "make him look better" in court. She told the jury, "He said the way I chose my words, my demeanor and tone of voice would have a lot to do with whether he was convicted or not."

The spectators sat with rapt attention as Michael's ex-wife admitted she and Michael had been married four years when she agreed to go along with Michael's plan to have an affair with Kathryn so he could obtain a loan for his failing scuba shop. She admitted she created false documents to show the scuba shop had more income than it actually did. What she did not count on was Michael divorcing her to marry Kathyrn. However, she admitted that she and Michael had an affair after he married Kathyrn. She told the court she lied to the police when they questioned her about her continued involvement with Michael. She said she initially wanted to protect Michael because she was still in love with him, but that was no longer the case.

A friend of Kathyrn's, Kathy Kolstad, told the court, "The guy was fascinating. I could see how happy she [Kathyrn] was, and after you talked to him, you could get past his appearance." Kathy said when she first met Michael, he mentioned he had worked as a page under the Johnson Administration and as an ambassador to a small African nation. Michael told Kathy the U.S. Department of State had him on a retainer for matters of defense.

Kathy told how Michael would get phone calls in the middle of the night and would have to take the calls outside for "security reasons." She recalled that he told her he began scuba diving after he graduated from Harvard University. The couple told Kathy they planned to get married in Hawaii and then spend a year on Easter Island. Kathryn planned to take a leave from her job so she could accompany Michael as he led seventy-five members of a National Geographic scuba team on an expedition.

Kathy summed up her thoughts on Michael by saying, "The man was a genius. He knew facts and figures and details that only someone who has been there or has done extensive research would know." She told the court she "absolutely" believed what Michael told her about his background.

Michael chose to take the witness stand in his own defense. He began by saying, "I lied repeatedly to the police. I did not want to be arrested. I did not want to be accused of murdering my wife." District Attorney Barnes asked Michael if he would lie "to get off on this murder charge?" Michael readily agreed, "I'm sure I probably would. I probably would at one point—I wouldn't now." Michael told the jury that in the past he had lied to his wife, his accountant, his attorney, his minister, and the police. He admitted he had lied with a straight face for "probably as long as I can remember."[6] Michael told the jury that he originally began dating Kathryn in order to use her to get a business loan for his scuba shop.

The defense called Dr. Philip Barnhart, who had interviewed Michael on three occasions after his arrest. He described Michael as an intelligent man "who operates [emotionally] as if empty. He said Michael clearly fit the criteria of a narcissistic personality and was manipulative, preoccupied with fantasies, an exhibitionist and "highly nonconforming." Dr. Barnhart went onto say that Michael had almost no ability to understand how his exploitative actions harm other people. He added, "Mr. Lissy has demonstrated he is not a particularly empathetic person toward other people. In fact, that's an understatement. He does not exhibit that tendency at all." Dr. Barnhart told the jury Michael was "clearly schizophrenic and very, very disturbed." Before leaving the witness stand, Dr. Barnhart said, "Lissy has sometimes become so absorbed in his personal fantasies that he doesn't realize what's going on around him."[7]

In his closing remarks, District Attorney Barnes reminded the jury that Michael had admitted he had lied to everyone and had fantasied about murder plots. He told the jury Michael admitted to stealing from his previous employers, defrauding insurance companies, and defrauding the Internal Revenue Service. He also admitted to a robbery, a burglary, and dealing drugs. Looking at the jury he said, "If he's guilty, find him guilty of aggravated murder. If he's not, let him go. Let him take his insurance money and run." The final question he put before the jury was: "Did they believe Lissy when he said he never intended to have his wife killed to collect insurance money?"

Michael's defense attorney rejected the entire notion that Michael hired a hitman to murder his wife. Although he had earlier referred to his client as "morally despicable," he told the jury Kathryn was "more of an asset alive than dead to Lissy. Never in any of these schemes has he ever intended the death of another human being ... he's a victim of his own mouth."

It took the jury six hours to return a verdict of guilty of aggravated murder. Michael was sentenced to life in prison, with a mandatory thirty year minimum. Kathyrn's mother told the *Corvallis Gazette-Times*, "We'll never get over the loss of her, but at least we've seen justice prevail. She was one joyous young person." David pled guilty to aggravated murder and conspiracy to commit murder. He received a sentence of life in prison.

Gretchen was charged with aggravated murder. She accepted a plea bargain and pled guilty to conspiracy to commit murder and robbery. She admitted driving David to and from the Valley River Inn. Her defense attorney, John Halpern, Jr., asked the court for probation due to her age and lack of a criminal record. He believed Gretchen was a good candidate for rehabilitation. Lane County Circuit Judge Edwin Allen sentenced Gretchen to forty years in prison. He imposed a mandatory term of ten years on each count, for a total of twenty years of mandatory imprisonment. Judge Allen stated his reason for the lengthy sentence:

> This defendant has shown by her actions that she is willing to commit murder for hire, one of the most damnable, aggravated crimes that there is. One of the most callous aspects of the crime was Schumacher's admission to police that after she and Wilson returned to Portland the night of the murder, they sold a gold and diamond necklace taken from Martini-Lissy to a drug dealer for methamphetamine.

Michael settled into his life behind bars. In Michael's second Christmas inside the prison walls, he donned a Santa Claus suit and entertained the children who came to visit the prison. He was actually substituting for a fellow inmate who usually played the part of Santa Claus but who had come down with the flu. It was the first time the prison allowed visitors on Christmas Day. Michael told Peter Sleeth of the *Statesman Journal*:

> It's an emotional high, that is hard to explain. One kid had wanted a G.I. Joe doll for two years. We gave it to him, and tears just came pouring down his face. Even old Santa had tears coming out. We've all taken a lot out of the community, and it's our chance to put something back.[8]

Michael told Peter that Christmas was an unemotional time for him on the outside, but now as Santa Claus, he is learning to believe in Christmas.

Michael's attorney filed an appeal arguing that it was illegal for the police to use a wiretap to secretly record Michael speaking on the telephone and it was illegal for them to record a face-to-face meeting with a witness.

Two years after Michael's trial, the Oregon Supreme Court ruled that police do not need court orders to record telephone conversations, as long as one party is aware they are being recorded and as long as they are not coerced. The decision upheld the ruling that police can use wiretaps in murder for hire cases. They stated that the state law is stricter than federal law, in that the state law requires a court order, but the federal law does not, as long as one of the party consents to the recording.

7

Julie Ann Salter

On September 24, 1980, detectives from the Clackamas County Sheriff's Office were dispatched to a homicide of a thirty-two-year-old female in Lake Oswego. Once on scene, they found Julie Anne Salter, dead from a single gunshot wound to the head. Her body was located outside of her house. The detectives did not have much to go on. They learned Julie had been married to James Salter, a prominent attorney in Seattle. The marriage had ended on a bad note with a bitter custody battle over their six-year-old daughter.

The Clackamas County Sheriff's Office had worked eight homicides during the summer; more than they usually worked in an entire year. They tried to establish a link between the murder of Julie to any of the other murders, but they came up empty handed.

Two years later, what began as a routine robbery case, led the Seattle Police Department to not one, but two, murder for hire plots. David Alwin told Seattle Police Detective Al Smalley that three men held him at gunpoint in his house and robbed him of $25 and a small amount of cocaine. Investigators pieced together that Christopher Tine, age twenty-five, Robert Haden King, Jr., age thirty-one, and Warren Theophilus "Teddy" Hill, age thirty-five, were responsible for robbing David.

The detectives finally got the break they needed. The Seattle Police Department brought Teddy in to question him about the robbery. They were asking him questions about the robbery, when he mentioned the contract murder of Julie Slater. Teddy told the detectives Robert Haden King promised him $15,000 to murder Julie. Teddy said he had only received $10,000. He said the order for Julie's murder came from her ex-husband, James. Robert had been a private investigator for Julie's husband's law firm. Teddy explained to the detectives that it was Robert who contacted him with the proposal of a murder for hire.

From there, things came together quickly and arrest warrants were issued for Teddy Hill and Robert King for the murder of Julie Anne Salter. They were now facing a charge of aggravated murder. Teddy had been in trouble with the law in Alabama. He served time for larceny and forgery. He was also convicted of manslaughter and served seven years in Alabama for that crime before moving to Oregon.

Robert grew up with Teddy in Gadsden, Alabama. Robert graduated from Gadsden High School and went onto to earn a marketing degree from the University of Colorado. He earned a law degree from the University of Baltimore Law School in 1977. His father was a prominent attorney in Gadsden. Robert married a woman who was from Seattle. Robert's name had recently been mentioned when Benjamin Bullitt, the heir to the KING Broadcasting Company drowned in the dark waters of Lake Washington.

Robert was Benjamin's financial advisor. In 1981, Benjamin paid $360,000 for a 67-foot yacht he named *Pegasus*. The day after purchasing the yacht, Benjamin and his friends took the yacht out on Lake Washington. That night, Benjamin decided to jump into the water after spending the day drinking alcohol and doing cocaine. Benjamin was never seen or heard from again. The U.S. Coast Guard sent a helicopter to aid the Harbor Patrol. The twenty-four-year-old heir was presumed drowned. His body was never found. The police were never able to tie Robert to being on the yacht the day Benjamin drowned.

The investigators learned Robert had been arrested for allegedly filing a false insurance claim totaling $68,000 when he lived in Baltimore. That arrest prohibited him from taking the bar exam in Alabama. Once he was off probation, Robert and his wife moved to Gadsden but were not there long before deciding to move to Seattle.

Once the young couple settled in Seattle, they began running in circles with affluent people. After learning of Robert's arrest, one of Robert's friends told a reporter, "Looking at it in retrospect, he was a well-mannered guy, real polite, who came on with a highly educational mock-up in business and law. His personality spoke with a lot of authority and power."

As the detectives were working on the armed robbery case, they learned Robert, Teddy, and Conrad William Terry were in the process of planning a murder for hire on Ole Pedersen. Ole owned a successful jewelry business in Seattle. Ole was married to Gwen Pedersen, but Gwen was having an affair with Conrad. The three men decided to murder Ole so Conrad could marry Gwen and they could share his estate.

Robert, Teddy, and Conrad were arrested and charged with conspiracy to commit murder in the first degree. They each pled innocent to the charge. They were held in jail on $100,000 bond. Lieutenant Bob Holter of the Seattle Police Department told reporters, "We now have the primary players in custody."

Robert and Teddy's trial for conspiracy to commit murder got underway three months after their arrest, but before the attorneys had a chance to give their opening remarks, Robert threatened a witness for the prosecution. As the jail guard led Robert down the hallway to the courtroom, Robert saw a former business partner and uttered two words: "You're dead."

Gwen's statement to the police was introduced into evidence. She had told the investigators she was having an affair with Conrad but had refused to divorce her husband and marry Conrad, as he had suggested. King County Deputy District Attorney William Redkey told the jury:

> King and Terry talked and it was decided King would arrange to have Mr. Pedersen out of the picture. Then supposedly what would happen is that Terry would marry the former Mrs. Pedersen, who would inherit the estate. King would get ten percent of the estate.[1]

Deputy District Attorney Redkey told the court that Gwen did not know about the murder plot. He went on to say Conrad told the police he changed his mind about murdering Ole but Robert told him it was too late to back out. He said the plan was in motion and could not be stopped.

The jurors listened as the details were explained. Deputy District Attorney Redkey said Robert offered to pay Teddy $8,000 to murder Ole. The first $2,000 would be paid up front. He explained that Robert then brought four other men into the plot. Their job was to stalk Ole for the next three months. Robert allegedly gave the explanation that he was owed money by Ole and he needed the foursome to stalk him and report back.

Seattle Police Department Lieutenant Bob Holter told the jury that the day came and Robert, Teddy, and one of the other men piled into a car and drove towards Ole's jewelry store with the intention of murdering Ole. He said Robert pulled a sawed-off shotgun out of his duffle bag. An argument ensued, a scuffle took place, and the gun went off. It damaged the back seat of the car but no one was injured. Fearing they had called attention to themselves, the trio decided against committing the murder that night.

Lieutenant Holter told the jury that when the police learned of the potential murder, they informed Ole, who decided to leave Washington state. It only took the jury four hours to convict both men of conspiracy to commit murder. Weeks later, they were both convicted of the armed robbery of David Alwin. Their next stop was Oregon. Robert appeared before Judge Dale M. Jacobs and stated that he would be acting as his own attorney. He agreed to having a court-appointed lawyer to be his co-counsel.

Teddy's trial got underway quickly. Prosecutor Dennis Miller told the jury, "This was not a crime of passion, this was a crime for money." Teddy's statement to the police was introduced into evidence. At the time of his arrest, he told the detectives that Robert agreed to pay him $15,000 to murder Julie. Teddy said a man by the name of Mike drove him to Lake Oswego to commit the murder. He admitted to the police that he killed Julie by shooting her in the head one time. Mike then drove him back to Seattle and they buried the murder weapon in the woods. Teddy told the investigators that Robert only paid him $10,000 after the murder. It took the jury less than two hours to return a verdict of guilty of aggravated murder. Teddy was sentenced to life imprisonment.

As part of a plea bargain, Robert agreed to testify against James. Robert appeared before the Clackamas County grand jury and testified that James had hired him to kill his ex-wife. After listening to all of the testimony, the grand jury indicted James on a charge of aggravated murder.

Julie's ex-husband, James, who had worked as an attorney since graduating from law school, now found himself needing an attorney. He was arrested at his home in Seattle, three years after his ex-wife was murdered. James was brought to Portland and placed in a different jail than Robert, in an effort to keep the two separated. He was held without bail until a bail hearing could be arranged.

At the bail hearing, Robert testified James wanted his wife, "raped, and stabbed and cut-up, before she was killed." A week later, Circuit Judge Patrick Gilroy set James' bail at $250,000. He told the attorneys, "The court is unable to make the finding requested by the state that the defendant be denied bail. My decision in this makes no finding [of] Mr. Salter's guilt or innocence." James posted the required ten percent of $250,000 and was able to return home after thirty-five days in jail.

Part of Robert's plea bargain was that he was to testify not only in front of the grand jury, but also, at James' trial. However, on the day he was scheduled to testify at James' trial, he appeared to be less than capable of doing so. As the guard led him into the courtroom, the jury and spectators noticed he was barefoot, and wearing a bulletproof vest over a torn T-shirt and sweatpants. He took the witness stand, but kept grabbing his head and rocking back and forth. He began crying and saying his head hurt. He told Judge Patrick Gilroy that he could not remember why he was in the courtroom.

Robert's attorney, William "Tim" Lyons, submitted reports from two psychiatrists that said Robert was "in an active psychotic state." Tim asked Judge Gilroy that Robert be excused from testifying. Judge Gilroy spoke to the jail guards that had dealt with Robert prior to his court appearance. The guards indicated Robert had been fine earlier in the day. Judge Gilroy told Tim, "I think he's faking it ... He should testify."

With that, Robert did take the witness stand. He told the jury James had told him he wanted his ex-wife dead and he would pay $25,000 for that to happen. James allegedly told Robert that he wanted Julie dead, so he could gain sole custody of their daughter. Robert recalled the first time James mentioned his desire to have his ex-wife killed was approximately six months before the murder took place. At that time, he told James that he would make arrangements for the murder to take place. He told the jury, "But I really wasn't going to do it. I was just going to make some money off Jim." As James became more persistent, Robert agreed to help him with his plan. Robert told the jury, "I told him I wouldn't do it, but I knew somebody I could get to do it. I knew I could get Teddy Hill to do it ... Teddy killed people for a living."[2]

The child psychiatrist who interviewed James, Julie, and their daughter, during their divorce proceedings, was called to the witness stand. Dr. John E. Dunne of Seattle told the court Julie had called James a pathological liar and said she could no longer trust him. Dr. Dunne said he asked James about the accusations and James explained that his lying could be considered more like exaggerating the details, not actually lying. James did tell Dr. Dunne, "That he had to almost compulsively tell the truth because once he started into a lie, he could not stop." Dr. Dunne told the court James wanted to overcome this problem.

A former law partner of James, Shirley Fox, took the witness stand and said Robert had informed her that James hired him to murder Julie. She told the court their conversation took place two days after Julie was murdered. Although Shirley did not believe Robert, she did ask him why he would do such a thing. She recalled Robert saying James was going to pay him $25,000 from the life insurance proceeds. James took the witness stand in his own defense. He vehemently told the court he never hired anyone to harm Julie. He emphasized, "I would never have wanted to have Julie murdered." He also stated he had never met Teddy.

James' trial dragged on for seven weeks. A total of ninety-nine witnesses took the stand. The jury was shown more than five hundred exhibits. During the closing arguments, Clackamas County Deputy District Attorney Terry Gebolys told the jury James was, "a liar, a cheat, a con man and a murderer. This is not a case that jumps out at anybody and says, 'Jim Salter did it.' Someone as cunning and intelligent as Mr. Salter would never leave a trail for you to look at. His trail has many curves, lots of sidetracks and lots of coverups." Deputy District Attorney Gebolys told the jury when they put all the pieces together, "they point a direct finger at James Salter."[3]

Speaking to the reason James allegedly wanted his ex-wife murdered, District Attorney Gebolys stated, "He knew he couldn't get custody legally, so he did what he had to do in order to obtain custody illegally, and he did that through Bob King and Teddy Hill."[4]

James' defense attorney, Kenneth Morrow of Eugene, began his closing remarks by telling the jury, "You folks are being asked to swallow some explanations that are absolutely unbelievable." He stressed Robert was framing James in an effort to save himself. He referred to Robert as a liar and a con man. He reminded the jury Robert had been involved with drugs and insurance fraud.

Finally, it was time for the jury to begin deliberations. After seven hours of deliberations, they returned with a verdict that shocked the courtroom. James was found innocent. Ten members of the jury had voted for an acquittal; two members voted guilty. The majority vote was enough to send him home. James put his heads in his hands and began to cry. He and Kenneth were taken out of the courtroom by guards who feared something might happen if they did not remove them quickly.

Later, a juror who asked to remain anonymous told reporters, "The state just didn't have enough evidence, in my opinion, to prove it beyond a reasonable doubt, although there were some questions in everybody's minds." James told reporters from the Associated Press:

> Obviously I'm very pleased. Justice has prevailed. What can I say? I'm elated. I'm relieved. I'm looking forward to a long and prosperous life and I'm proud of the jury ... The last time I cried this much was when Julie died. But that was a cry of despair. This is a cry of joy. I can't deny that I feared they would find me guilty, but I wouldn't have believed it. I'm glad they saw through King. Now I will try to reestablish my life and will wait for my baby to be born.[5]

James had remarried after divorcing Julie. His new wife adopted the daughter he shared with Julie. Once the trial was over, the three of them settled into their home and awaited the new baby's arrival two months later.

It was now time for Robert to stand trial for the murder of Julie. Early on, Robert had accepted a plea deal, wherein he would testify against James in exchange for the state dropping the charge of aggravated murder. Robert agreed to pled guilty to a charge of murder, thus eliminating the mandatory thirty year minimum sentence. After James was acquitted, Robert decided he would gamble and put his case before a jury, in the hopes, that he too would be found innocent.

Robert's trial got underway with Clackamas County Circuit Judge Dale Jacobs presiding. His defense attorney was Tim Lyons, who had represented him during James' trial. Chief Deputy District Attorney S. Dennis Miller represented the state of Oregon. The jury was made up of seven men and five women, with two alternates. Each juror had been questioned privately about how much they knew about the case due to the extensive media coverage.

Philip DeTurk, an attorney from Seattle, told the court Robert suffered from brain damage. He explained that Robert had been in a private plane that crashed in Tennessee a few years prior. He explained that Robert and his friends were planning on going wild boar hunting in Tennessee when the plane went down. Dr. Harvey Ries, of the Fairfax Psychiatric Hospital in Kirkland, Washington had recently diagnosed Robert as suffering from "organic brain syndrome with amnesia."

The trial came to a screeching halt when a witness for the prosecution alluded to Robert having been involved in murders that took place in Colorado. Robert's attorney immediately requested a mistrial. Judge Jacobs scheduled a hearing to determine if a mistrial was warranted. In the end, he declared a mistrial.

Shortly thereafter, a new trial got underway. Five days before the fourth anniversary of Julie's murder, the jury found Robert guilty of aggravated murder. He was sentenced to life in prison with a minimum of thirty years before being eligible for parole. The sentence was to run consecutively with his conviction for conspiracy to commit murder in Washington state. Three years after Robert was found guilty, the Court of Appeals upheld his aggravated murder conviction.

8

Rice Family

"I thought these things only happened in the movies or maybe in some city like Chicago. I couldn't believe it was happening to us." Those were the words spoken by Richard Rice after learning that a hit had been put out for him, his girlfriend, and her four-year-old son.

In late November 1979, newspapers across the country carried the news of the "mysterious disappearance" of a family in Oregon. Richard Rice, age thirty-four,

Sharon Morgan, age twenty-four, and her four-year-old son, were supposed to be traveling from Redmond to Turner. When they failed to show up at Richard's brother's house in Turner, he contacted the Redmond Police Department. The Redmond Police Department requested the assistance from the Oregon State Police and the Deschutes County Sheriff's Office. Trooper Ron Benckendorf, of the Oregon State Police, told the *Statesman Journal*, "We have no idea where anyone is or where to start looking."

Missing persons bulletins were distributed to law enforcement agencies. The family's car was located in a parking lot in Bend days after they had been reported missing. That only added to the speculation of what had happened to the family of three. Suddenly people everywhere were talking about the missing family.

In reality, the family was alive and well, having been secreted away by agents from the U.S. Bureau of Alcohol, Tobacco and Firearm (ATF). Days after the family disappeared, a man by the name of Therron Austin "Bob" Johnson was arrested by the U.S. marshals and charged with conspiracy to commit murder. He was booked into the Maricopa County Jail in Phoenix, Arizona.

After Bob's arrest, Richard phoned his brother, and simply said they were "safe and accounted for" and would see him in a few days. Richard hung up the phone before his brother could ask any details. Richard's brother informed the police that he had heard from his brother.

When the media reported this, it only added to the curiosity of the people who had been following the story. Reporters at the *Statesman Journal* figured out that Bob had lived in Salem and Lyons. He was the previous owner of the Marion Forks restaurant in Idanha. They learned at one time Bob had been married to Sharon's ex-mother-in-law, Dorothy Morgan. Before Dorothy married Bob, she was married to Vern Morgan. Their son, Jim, was Sharon's ex-husband. Bob and Vern had been business partners in a timber company. Bob was convicted of timber theft in 1971 and given a five-year suspended prison sentence. The reporters learned Richard was employed as a lumber broker.

Armed with their research, the *Statesman Journal* contacted the Portland Bureau of the ATF. ATF Agent Robert Acord confirmed Bob's arrest involved the missing Redmond family. Beyond that, he would only say "no comment."

Bob was released on bail after posting $11,000. When Richard's brother found out that Bob was no longer behind bars, he was concerned. He told reporters, "I've been told they're safe and I guess I have to keep believing that until I find out something else."

Reporter Cynthia Jabs of the *Oregon Statesman Reporter* spoke to Richard's mother. She said she had been informed by "authorities" that the family was safe and in protective custody. She would not reveal who had given her that information. She added, "It takes a lot to convince a mother."

A few days after Bob posted bail, agents with the Los Angeles Bureau of the ATF arrested Harold "Chopper" Covey, age fifty, and charged him with conspiracy to commit murder. The agents believed Harold was the person who had previously tried to kill Richard. Once Harold was behind bars, the agents allowed Richard, Sharon, and her son to return to their home in Redmond. As it turned out, when the ATF agents whisked them away from danger, they placed them at a ranch Richard's parents owned outside of Burns. The couple spent twelve days at the ranch trying to figure out who would want to harm them. The agents informed Richard there had been a previous attempt on his life when someone fired a rifle at him. Richard was unaware of the attempt on his life.

The ATF released a few details to the media. They explained that the case began in Oklahoma where Bob tried to hire a hitman. What Bob did not know was that he was actually talking to an undercover ATF agent. Bob met the undercover agent in Arizona, where Bob allegedly paid the undercover agent $6,000 to plant a bomb in Richard's car.

The ATF kept their cards close to their chest but did say the investigation centered on Oregon. Lee Peters of the ATF told *The Capital Journal*, "I've had half a dozen calls from people with leads we're pursuing. We're still exploring every possible angle, and there probably are some that haven't come to our attention yet." The ATF admitted to planting Richard's car in the parking lot in Bend as part of their "disappearance charade."[1]

Cynthia Jabs of the *Oregon Statesman Reporter* was granted an interview with Richard and Sharon once they returned home. Richard said, "It felt like something out of a James Bond movie." He explained the first he heard about the murder for hire plot, was when ATF agents knocked on his door the day after Thanksgiving. He allowed them into his house when they explained their reason for being at his house.

The agents played a tape recording that covered more than one hour of people talking about the murder for hire plot. The ATF agents explained to Richard and Sharon that Bob Therron paid a person he believed to be a hitman, $6,000 to plant a bomb in Richard's car. Richard told Cynthia, the agents gave them just enough time to pack a few clothes, some food, and toys for the four-year-old before they were escorted to a ranch owned by Richard's parents. He explained that his parents were the only people allowed to know about the murder for hire plot. Richard said they told Sharon's son they were all going on a hunting trip, which excited him.

Richard told how he and Sharon spent their time at the ranch, trying to figure out a possible motive for the contract murder:

> I kept going over and over it, wondering who'd go to all this trouble to have us dead. The funny part about it is I really don't know. You'd think if somebody hated you that much ... I've got some personal feelings and suspicions, but I don't think its fair to talk about them, I might be wrong.[2]

Sharon told Cynthia that she knew Bob, but said she had not had any dealings with him since her divorce from Jim three years before. She exclaimed, "How anybody thinks they've got a right to get rid of somebody, just like that."

Richard said he last saw Bob the previous May when he picked up two loads of lumber at the lumber company Richard owned. Richard did say Bob had only paid $500 of the $10,000 he owed for the lumber.

Harold was released on bail. Both he and Bob pled innocent to the charge of conspiracy to commit murder. Bob retained Attorney John Flynn of Phoenix, Arizona to represent him. In the 1960s, John made national news when he successfully argued before the U.S. Supreme Court that a defendant has the right to remain silent when questioned by the police and to have an attorney present before being questioned.

The case began in 1963 when an eighteen-year-old woman was walking home from a bus stop in Phoenix. She had just completed working a shift at a movie theater. She was grabbed from behind and forced into the backseat of a car. She was driven to the outskirts of town and raped before being released. Days later, the girl and her cousin noticed a car driving in her neighborhood that she believed was the suspect's. The car was traced to a woman in Mesa, Arizona. That woman's boyfriend was Ernesto Miranda.

Ernesto agreed to accompany the police back to their headquarters to appear in a police line-up. The victim was unable to identify the suspect. Nevertheless, the police questioned Ernesto for two hours without an attorney present. Ernesto signed a written confession, which was the only evidence in the case. Ernesto was convicted. His attorney, Alvin Moore, appealed the conviction to the Arizona Supreme Court with the concern that Ernesto's statement to the police was not made voluntarily.

The Arizona Supreme Court ruled that Ernesto was aware of his constitutional rights when he signed the confession. Soon after, the American Civil Liberties Union became aware of the case. Attorney Robert Corcoran asked trial lawyer John Flynn to get involved in the case. John was assisted by a constitutional lawyer, John Frank.

In 1966, the U.S. Supreme Court reversed the Arizona Supreme Court's decision. Chief Justice Earl Warren wrote a sixty-page opinion that outlined proper police procedure to ensure every suspect is aware of their rights once they are detained by the police. The now famous Miranda warning is used by every police officer in the United States. The verbiage varies from one jurisdiction to another but the crux is:

> You have the right to remain silent. Anything you say can and will be used against you in a court of law. You have the right to speak to an attorney and have him present with you while you are being questioned. If you cannot afford an attorney, one will be provided for you. Do you understand the rights I just read to you? With these rights in mind, do you wish to speak to me?

If a defendant is not given their Miranda warning, their statement may be inadmissible in a court of law.

Even with a famous attorney representing him, Bob decided to plead guilty to solicitation to commit murder. Harold also pled guilty to the charge. Harold was sentenced to three years, nine months in prison. Bob was sentenced to eight years in prison. The motive for the murder for hire was never revealed.

9

When the Person Posing as a Hitman is Really an Undercover Cop

After a difficult divorce, William DeRousse mentioned to his employees that he wanted to hire a hitman to murder his wife. William, age fifty-seven, and his wife, Laureen, age twenty-seven, had been embroiled in a bitter divorce and custody battle over their child. William's employees went to the authorities with this information. Polk County Sheriff's Office sent Deputy Paul Burke to meet William at the Eola Inn Restaurant in Salem. Paul was dressed in street clothes and never gave away his true identity.

During the meeting, William allegedly agreed to pay Deputy Burke $1,000 to murder his wife. Half of the money was to be paid up front. William allegedly told Deputy Burke the money was in his car, which was out in the parking lot. As they left the restaurant to go to William's car, Deputy Burke gave a signal to a detective waiting in the parking lot. Polk County Detective George Morgan approached William and placed him under arrest as he counted the money.

William was freed on bail. He pled innocent due to being legally insane at the time of the incident. His trial was postponed after it was decided he needed to undergo psychiatric examinations. William had been arrested months before for custodial interference. He allegedly removed his child from the Polk County Courthouse during his divorce hearing with Laureen. After that arrest, he was released on his own recognizance.

Six months after the meeting at the restaurant, the trial got underway in the Polk County Circuit Court with Judge Darrell Williams presiding. Polk County District Attorney John Snyder represented the state of Oregon. Charles Burt represented William.

In his opening remarks, District Attorney Snyder told the court William's actions to solicit a murder for hire, "was premeditated. It was not done on the spur of the moment ... he was very businesslike." This was not William's first marriage, he explained; it was actually his fifth. District Attorney Snyder expanded that William had a history of rage and anger, "But he is not mentally deficient to the point that it should excuse him. He is not psychotic."

Jurors learned William had been treated at the Oregon State Mental Hospital in 1971 as ordered by the court on a previous case. Since that time, he had been taking lithium to treat what doctors at the Oregon State Mental Hospital diagnosed as manic depression. Charles then told the jury, "But a manic depressive with a twist—he's always manic. He's hyperactive. He had been a man possessed—unable to stop working." Charles said it was not unusual for William to work sixteen hours a day.

Dr. John Carter of Eugene testified he had been treating William for his manic depression for the past few months. When William's attorney questioned Dr. Carter about William's state of mind at the time he allegedly tried to hire a hitman, Dr. Carter stated:

> At that time.... he was so affected by his mental disorder that it severely impaired his ability to control his action and conform his conduct to the requirements of law. He was unable to perceive the consequences of his actions. In my opinion, his ability to tell right from wrong, was severely impaired. It's conceivable he would have gone ahead and done it even if the officer had been in uniform ... people in extreme manic state make bizarre judgments.[1]

Dr. Carter went onto explain that William had been under tremendous stress due to the divorce and child custody battle. He explained the stress, "would tend to increase his emotional disorder. He would tend to lose control of his thought structure and have less and less access to good judgment."[2]

The next witness for the defense was Dr. Ruth Jens. She had been involved with the early studies of using lithium to treat mental illnesses. She told the jury, "Manic depressives are psychotic in the manic state. Their judgment is unable to keep up with their behavior. It happens in almost 100 percent of the cases."[3]

Polk County District Attorney John Snyder called Dr. Wesley Weissert to the witness stand. It was Weissert's testimony that William did not suffer from a mental disorder that would prevent him from being able to distinguish between right and wrong:

> I could find no evidence that he ever had a major mental illness. He'd had problems all his life, but not serious mental illness. It is my opinion that he does not have a mental disease where he is unable to perceive the criminality of his conduct.[4]

Charles questioned Dr. Weissert about how William's stress level could have been a barrier to him understanding the legal implications of his actions. Dr. Weissert simply said, "Even if he was in a manic state ... I would still say he was responsible."

The prosecution also called Dr. John Cochran to the witness stand. Dr. Cochran worked as a psychologist at the Oregon State Mental Hospital. He agreed that William was mentally ill but stated in his opinion, William "acted out of simple motives of rage and revenge." He told the jury William was capable of being responsible for his actions.

Polk County Deputy Burke told the jury about his meeting with William. He said it came about after William's employees contacted the Polk County Sheriff's Office. Deputy Burke said he presented himself to William as a "hitman." He recalled William seemed "nervous and a little afraid, but sure of himself. He said he wanted me to give his wife an overdose of heroin and get rid of her, or words to that effect."

Deputy Burke testified, "I told him I would do it my way—how it would be done was my business—and that it would be accomplished with 48 hours because I was leaving the state." He went onto say they agreed the price would be $1,000. William was to pay half up front, and half when Laureen was dead. Deputy Burke told the court he wrote a fictious name and address on a napkin and gave it to William with the instructions he was to send the remaining $500 once the murder was completed.

Deputy Burke explained they agreed to go out to William's car in the parking lot, where William would give him the first $500. Before leaving the restaurant, Deputy Burke asked William, "Once I walk out that door, your wife is dead. Is that what you want?" He said William answered, "Yes."

Once William was in handcuffs, he asked why he was under arrest. When told it was for solicitation for murder, William allegedly said, "All I asked you to do is get my daughter back; I just wanted you to kidnap my daughter." Deputy Burke testified that in his opinion, William did not appear to be under the influence of any drugs. He stated he was very familiar with the signs of drug use from his work in law enforcement.

Charles cross examined Deputy Burke and pointed out in Deputy Burke's testimony, he quoted William as referring to kidnapping his daughter. Charles explained that the child in the custody dispute was a boy, not a girl.

William's employees told the jury that William had repeatedly stated he wanted, "to have his wife dead. He said he was either going to kill her himself or have someone else kill her. He said he hated her, and he became insistent that we find someone to kill her." They also told the jury William told them, "He would just act crazy for a while and plead insanity, then get out after a few years and live. He said as long as she was alive, he couldn't live." They explained when he first mentioned his plan, they thought he was just upset and would get past it. However, they relayed, "He didn't. He just got worse."[5]

William took the stand in his own defense. He quickly explained that the meeting with the deputy had nothing to do with wanting to have his wife murdered, but instead was to find out how he could get full custody of his child. He adamantly stated, "The purpose of going was to get full custody of my child."

William elaborated on his plan, saying it was his employees who had offered to set him up with the deputy. They told him they knew Deputy Burke from their own stints in prison, and that he was well connected with organized crime. William told the court his employees had offered to assist him gain sole custody of his child, in exchange for 20 percent ownership of a motel he owned.

It was his employees, William clarified, that gave him a "red pill" before driving him to the restaurant to meet with the deputy. William firmly denied ever asking Deputy Burke to murder Laureen. William expanded on the thought saying, it was Deputy Burke who asked if he wanted his wife killed, to which he firmly stated, "no." William flatly denied telling his employees that if he could not find a hitman, he would kill Laureen himself, as District Attorney Snyder told the jury in his opening remarks.

William's son from a previous relationship took the stand in his father's defense, as did his sister, and a friend. William's ex-wife, Laureen, told the jury she had tried to have William committed the previous summer due to his erratic behavior.

In his closing remarks, District Attorney Snyder told the jury, "You have to consider that if Mr. DeRousse hadn't been cornered, his wife would be dead today ... even if you accept that he's a manic depressive, it's not an excuse for his conduct."

The jury deliberated for two hours, then returned to the courtroom with a verdict of guilty of solicitation to commit murder. Judge Williams sentenced William to eight years in prison.

10
Patricia Osborne

In May 1980, Patricia Osborne died in a house fire in Lookingglass, just outside of Roseburg. From the start, things did not seem right to the investigators. They questioned if she had actually died in the fire. A medical examiner solidified their doubts when he confirmed Patricia was already dead when the fire broke out. The autopsy showed Patricia had been shot prior to the fire.

A year later, her husband, Walter Osborne, was arrested in Roseburg. At the same time, Danny Michael Saunders was arrested in California. They were charged with aggravated murder, murder, arson, and conspiracy to commit murder in the death of Patricia.

Patricia and Walter had recently divorced. The divorce had dragged on with bitter resentments on both sides. The couple had three young children. Witnesses told the authorities Walter had threatened to kill Patricia himself if he was unable to find someone else to do it. Danny was allegedly the hitman that Walter hired to kill Patricia and then set the house on fire in an effort to make it appear she had succumbed to the fire. Danny was the first to stand trial. It did not take the jury long to convict him of murder. He was sentenced to life in prison.

Two years after Patricia died, her ex-husband appeared in court facing a lifetime in prison for his role in her death. The trial had not progressed very far when Douglas County Circuit Judge Robert Stults collapsed in his chambers. He was rushed to the hospital. Klamath County Circuit Judge Ted Abram travelled to Roseburg to hear the motions for a mistrial. After listening to the testimony from the prosecutor and the defense attorney, Judge Abram declared a mistrial.

It was not long before the second trial began. One of the first orders of business for Circuit Judge Laurence Cushing was to study the previous rulings and briefs in the Osborne case. At hand was the question of Danny having to testify. After completing his research, Judge Cushing ruled Danny was required to testify, and refusing to do so would bring about a charge of contempt of court.

Douglas County Deputy District Attorney Howard Anderson began his opening remarks by telling the jury they would hear of a contract wherein Walter wanted Danny to murder his wife. He told the jurors Walter wanted his wife dead and was willing to pay for that to happen.

Defense Attorney Charles Burt represented the defendant. He readily told the jury that his client was innocent of all charges. He said Walter was not even in the area when Patricia died in the fire; he was on a fishing trip with his children and other family members at Diamond Lake.

In the first trial, Judge Stults had ruled the jury would not be allowed to hear a tape recording between Walter and Danny, in which Walter allegedly told Danny he would pay him $6,000 if he would murder Patricia. Danny stated he had received $1,200 from Walter. On the tape Danny allegedly admitted to shooting Patricia and then setting the house on fire. The second jury was allowed to hear the tape recording.

As the trial wrapped up, Deputy District Attorney Anderson reminded the jury Walter had arranged to take his children to Diamond Lake to go fishing to set up "a perfect alibi." He also spoke of the divorce that led to the murder for hire plot. He emphasized the medical examiner was able to determine Patricia was already dead when the fire was set. In his closing remarks, he asked the jury to return a verdict of guilty on all counts.

Charles told the jury Danny had lied when he admitted to killing Patricia and setting the house on fire. Referring to Danny's refusal to testify, Charles said, "He didn't have the guts to come into this courtroom, so he could be met face-to-face."

The day the jury began deliberations, the judge ordered that they be sequestered for the night to avoid hearing or reading any of the news accounts of the trial. They spent the night at a local hotel. The following day, they returned a verdict of guilty of murder, felony murder, arson, and conspiracy to commit murder. Walter immediately broke down and began sobbing. Walter was sentenced to life in prison for the murder for hire of his wife Patricia.

Charles said they would appeal based on the tape recording of Danny admitting to shooting Patricia that was admitted into evidence. Charles reminded the media that Judge Stults had ruled the tape recording as inadmissible, but Judge Cushing ruled that it could be admitted into evidence. It turned out the Court of Appeals ruled the tape recording should not have been introduced into evidence. They ordered that a new trial be held.

Two years later, Walter's third trial got underway. This time, the trial was held in Benton County at the request of Walter's attorney. Charles was concerned about the ability to select an unbiased jury in Douglas County after having already held two trials there. He had taken a poll of Douglas County residents and presented the findings to Judge Poole; the judge agreed to move the trial to Benton County.

Representing the State Department of Justice was Assistant Attorney General Douglas Dawson. Charles once again represented Walter. They jury was made up of eight women and four men. Judge Poole was the presiding judge. Charles contended, "No one can tell us how she died. There is no proof of how she died and you will never know." He put forth the possibilities that perhaps she had choked on a piece of meat, that she had overdosed on drugs, or had a heart attack. He told the jury that he could not solve the crime for them but reminded them his client was on a fishing trip with his children and family members at the time of Patricia's death.

The jury deliberated more than twenty-eight hours before returning a verdict. They acquitted Walter on all charges. Walter was overjoyed and began hugging his family members in the courtroom. As Walter walked out of the courtroom, a free man, he told the waiting reporters, "I just believe in the justice system. I believe it works. It just takes time. All I want to do now is go home and be with my kids now."

Patricia's mother, Thelma Kateley, said she was depressed, but she added, "But it's all right. I just feel sorry for the people who let a guilty man go free. The only satisfaction I get is knowing he spent some time in prison—and that's good. Nothing can ever bring my daughter back, and I just have to keep looking forward to life with my memories." Thelma described having to attend all three trials as "horrendous."[1]

The following year, Walter's brother, John, went on trial for his role in allegedly helping to arrange for a hitman to murder Patricia. John was found guilty on one count of murder and one count of felony murder.

Danny's brother Tom was convicted on conspiracy to commit murder for his role in the death of Patricia. He was paroled after serving less than five years.

After serving twenty-eight years for murder, Danny was determined to no longer be a danger to society and he was released from prison on the orders of the parole board. Yet before he could enjoy even an hour of freedom, he was immediately taken to the Douglas County Jail and booked into a jail cell. He was arrested for contempt of court based on his refusal to testify at Walter's second trial in 1985. He was ordered to serve one year on the contempt of court charge.

11
Killing a Hitman

On September 6, 2006, Susan Kuhnhausen returned home from work ready to relax after a long day. As she walked in the house, a stranger appeared, startling her. Suddenly, the man began swinging a hammer at her head. Susan immediately fought back, but the intruder was able to hit Susan several times in the head with the hammer before she was able to wrestle it away from him. The struggle continued with the two of them ending up on the floor. The intruder bit Susan several times but she was able to bite him back. Susan managed to get a chokehold on the intruder and was then able to strangle him using her bare hands. Once he was no longer a threat, she ran to her neighbor's house and asked them to phone the police.

The police arrived within minutes and found the intruder dead on Susan's hallway floor. Susan was treated for minor injuries at Providence Portland Medical Center and released. The police soon learned the identity of the intruder. He was fifty-nine-year-old Edward Dalton Haffey. The Multnomah County medical examiner determined the cause of death to be strangulation.

The investigators discovered Edward had a lengthy criminal record. He had previous convictions for conspiracy to commit murder, robbery, possession of burglary tools, and drug charges. The police concluded Susan was in her legal right to kill the intruder as self defense. They told the media they did not expect the case to go before a grand jury. They referred to the laws in Oregon that allow a person to use reasonable deadly force to defend themselves against an intruder or burglar in their own home.

As the investigation continued, the detectives gathered more information. Susan told them when she arrived home, the security alarm had been disabled. She explained that her soon-to-be ex-husband, Michael Kuhnhausen, was the only person who knew the alarm code, other than herself. She told the detectives Michael had let himself into the house earlier that day and left her a note indicating he was going to the beach. Susan told the detectives she believed Michael let Edward into the house so that he could kill her.

The police found a backpack that Edward had brought into Susan's house. Inside the backpack was a day planner. For the week of September 4, someone had written, "Call Mike, Get letter." Michael's cell phone number was written on the inside of a folder.

As the investigation unfolded, the detectives learned Edward had worked as a custodian at the Fantasy Adult Video Store, where Michael also worked. Michael was the person who had hired Edward. Within days of the attack, the Portland Police Bureau arrested Michael and charged him with conspiracy to commit murder and attempted murder.

Susan had worked at Providence Portland Medical Center as an emergency room nurse for thirty years. Her friends and family rallied around her. Susan left the following message on her answering machine in response to the volume of calls she was receiving:

> I'm not able to answer all the calls that I've received. I'm being comforted by your concern and your support. I want you to know that our lives are all at risk for random acts, but more likely random acts of love will come your way, than random acts of violence.

Michael pled not guilty to the charges against him. His bail was set at $2 million. At one of his hearings before Multnomah County Judge Frank Beardon, details about the pending divorce came to light. Michael's daughter from a previous marriage told the authorities Michael had recently purchased a .357 magnum handgun at a pawn shop. He had written a suicide note and left it for her weeks before. Multnomah County Deputy District Attorney Brian Davidson told the court, Michael had told his daughter's boyfriend that he could not face losing everything in a divorce. Brian relayed the information that Michael allegedly said, "anyone who would be willing to kill his wife would be well compensated."

Hearing this, Susan, who was attending the hearing, began sobbing. She later told Judge Beardon she had been living in fear of her life since the attack. She told the judge, "I don't think I should be forced into hiding." Michael's defense attorney, Donald Upham, told Judge Beardon, "There is no evidence, no proof period, that Mr. Kuhnhausen let this man into this house." Deputy District Attorney Davidson countered that Edward had told acquaintances, "He planned to kill a man's wife for $25,000 up front and $25,000 after he did the deed." He added that Michael's daughter had seen her father and Edward together days prior to the attack.

Judge Beardon reduced Michael's bail from $2 million down to $1 million. Michael's daughter posted the required ten percent of the bail so he could be released. The conditions of his release included that he be under house arrest and wear an ankle bracelet that would notify the authorities should he leave the house. The judge also made it clear he could not stay at his daughter's house because she was a witness in the case.

Michael made arrangements to stay with his son, but it turned out that was not possible. The son's landlord denied the son's request to have his father stay with him, owing to the fact he did not want the publicity. Michael was removed from his jail cell and was in the process of being released when he learned he had nowhere to go. He chose to return to his jail cell. The Department of Justice put out a statement, "In consultation with his attorney, he chose to return to jail rather than risk having his pretrial release revoked and be placed under arrest."

In the end, Michael pled guilty to solicitation to commit aggravated murder. Susan had the chance to speak at the sentencing hearing. She held up a photograph taken by the police the night of the attack. The photograph showed her face swollen, bloodied and bruised. Looking at Michael, she said, "You told the police that you found out I was okay. Do I look okay?" During her chance to speak, Susan also said, "I blame him in some measure for what he did, but I blame you more. As long as you live, I will never have a measure of peace. But I will not be destroyed." Four members of Susan's family and friends also addressed the court. Michael was sentenced to ten years in prison.

The Portland Police Bureau honored Susan with a Civilian Medal of Heroism. They mentioned her "sheer determination" and said, "Ms. Kuhnhausen has a peace-loving demeanor and has possessed a calm and assured composure throughout this arduous event."

Since the attack, Susan has devoted her life to helping victims. She has helped victims navigate the complex legal system and has been a pillar of strength for those who have been victims of crime. Referring to the attack, she had been quoted as saying:

> I immediately began to think about his family. Everybody has somebody who loves them. Children, a wife, a mother, a dad … the worst of this is not that somebody tried to kill me, but that I had to kill someone else to survive. But I have no shame because I did not choose this death for him. I chose my life. I chose life.

Susan continued to live in fear that Michael would hire another hitman. She moved out of the house where the attack occurred. Two years after the attack, Susan won a civil lawsuit against Michael. The civil trial lasted two days but Michael did not appear in person.

Michael died in prison just months before he was scheduled to be released. When asked by reporters her thoughts on Michael's death, Susan said, "I don't mourn his passing. Instead, I mourn the life he could have had, if only he could have opened his heart for those of us who cared about him."

12
Georgia Lee Dutton

When Susan Kuhnhausen strangled Edward Dalton Haffey, it was not the first time his name had been mentioned to law enforcement in Oregon. In 1991, the Lincoln Interagency Narcotics Team served a search warrant at a motel in Lincoln City and arrested Edward for manufacturing and possessing methamphetamine and being a felon in possession of a weapon. In the motel room, police located chemicals and equipment to manufacture methamphetamine. At the time of his arrest, he was in violation of his parole. He also had an active warrant from Lane County for burglary, theft, three counts of robbery, and three counts of conspiracy to commit robbery.

It was Edward's drug dealing that led him to be arrested for conspiracy to commit aggravated murder. In that particular case, Edward—along with John Michael Bray, age forty-eight, and William Earl Steiner, age twenty-one—allegedly plotted the death of Georgia Lee Dutton, age thirty-eight. Georgia and Edward were in a relationship but Georgia had threatened to go to the police with information about his involvement in the methamphetamine-manufacturing business.

In February 1991, Georgia was reported missing by her family. Weeks later, her body was pulled from the Umpqua River near Roseburg. An autopsy revealed she had been strangled to death. She had a high level of methamphetamine in her body at the time of her death.

A year later, John and William were arrested during a raid on a large-scale methamphetamine manufacturing operation near Salem. Investigators with the Polk Combined Agency Selective Enforcement Team received information that John, William, and Edward were involved in Georgia's death. William admitted to the investigators that the trio had been planning to murder Georgia for a month prior to carrying out their plan. Their reason for doing so, was that Georgia had threatened to tell the police that they were manufacturing and dealing methamphetamine. William told the enforcement team Georgia had been killed on a remote road near Buell. He said both he and John raped Georgia before William strangled her to death. He said they then placed her body in her motorhome and drove it to Roseburg where they dumped the body in the Umpqua River.

John, William, and Edward were arrested and charged with aggravated murder. Polk County Sheriff Ray Steele told the media, "Law enforcement is finding that large-scale drug operations are, more and more, leading into investigations of other crimes that involve weapons, stolen property, crimes of violence and murder."[1]

William and Edward agreed to testify against John in exchange for lesser sentences. Their sentencing was postponed until after they completed testifying. John was represented by defense attorney Jim Susee of Salem. Polk County District Attorney Fred Avera represented the state of Oregon. In Jim's opening remarks, he told the jury his client did not like Georgia, but had no reason to kill her. He admitted John was guilty of covering up the murder once he became aware of it, but that he did not participate in the rape or the murder. John, he explained, was behind the wheel of Georgia's motorhome when she was strangled to death by William.

District Attorney Avera opened the case by saying John and William had gone to Georgia's home, picked her up and driven her to a remote spot near Mill Creek Park. He went onto say John and William raped her and then William strangled her while John cheered him on. He said they placed the body in her motorhome and drove it to Roseburg where they disposed of the body in the Umpqua River.

Both William and Edward testified against John as they had agreed to do in their plea bargain. On the witness stand, William admitted to strangling Georgia while John watched. As the jury began deliberations, four questions were put before them. If John were to receive the death penalty, all twelve jurors had to agree on the following questions: Was the murder unprovoked? Was it deliberate? Was John a continuing threat to society? Should the defendant John Michael Bray receive the death penalty?

After deliberating for more than five hours, the jury voted unanimously on the first three questions. One juror voted against question number four, thus sparing John from the death penalty. John was found guilty of aggravated murder. He was sentenced to life in prison without the possibility of parole.

William pled guilty to aggravated murder in exchange for a sentence of life in prison with the possibility of parole after thirty years. Edward pled guilty to conspiracy to commit aggravated murder in exchange for a sentence of twelve years in prison.

13

Trying to Hire a Hitman

A simple theft of some aluminum cans turned into a murder for hire plot. In 2014, Dustin Kimbrough, age thirty-four, received a sentence of twenty years in prison for attempting to hire a hitman.

Two years prior, Dustin found himself behind bars after stealing some aluminum cans. He was charged with theft and burglary. He was in possession of methamphetamine when the police arrested him, which was a violation of his parole from a previous burglary charge. He was convicted and returned to prison.

Dustin was not in prison long before he began thinking of ways to kill his father-in-law, his brother-in-law, and Wasco County District Attorney Eric Nisley, who had prosecuted him on an earlier case. Dustin asked his cellmate, Francis Crowley if he would be willing to murder all three people. Francis readily agreed, thinking he could turn state's evidence and walk out of prison a free man. The two cellmates began plotting the murder for hire. When Francis was out of earshot of Dustin, he told a prison guard of their plans.

The prison authorities told Francis they would not take the threat seriously unless he had hard evidence. Francis returned to his cell and encouraged Dustin to put everything in writing. Dustin ended up writing fifty-three notes to Francis, all outlining his intentions to have the three individuals murdered.

In one of Dustin's many notes, he offered to pay Francis $80,000 to kill all three people. He promised to pay Francis out of the life insurance proceeds he would benefit from when his father-in-law died. He also wrote that Francis could steal valuables from his father-in-law after the murder and sell those items for cash.

A trial was held with Senior Assistant Attorney General Bumjoon Park representing the state. Amy Margolis represented Dustin. Francis took the witness stand and testified against Dustin. Members of Dustin's family told the court Dustin was a drug addict and needed help. Each member of Dustin's family testified they were in fear of Dustin, after learning of the murder for hire plot. They each mentioned they were still under a lot of stress.

Senior Assistant Attorney General Park told the court, "The amount of thought, hate, and malice towards these victims that was seething in his mind and heart ... was pretty frightening." After Dustin was sentenced to twenty years in prison, his attorney said they would appeal based on the fact the alleged note was never delivered to an actual hitman.

14
Three Hitmen—Three Unsuccessful Attempts

An arrest warrant for Sarah Aline Ater, age thirty, was issued in July 1999. An all-points bulletin was issued asking all law enforcement agencies to be on the lookout for Sarah. Sarah's attorney contacted the Multnomah County Jail and said his client would turn herself in. She did turn herself in, but she waited almost a day to do so. Sarah's picture had been plastered over the news and the media was covering her story with a great deal of interest. Benton County District Attorney Scott Heiser told the media, "We had a system-wide attempt to locate her. We were actively seeking her."

Sarah was booked into Multnomah County Jail and charged with ten felony counts. These included conspiracy to commit aggravated murder, soliciting aggravated murder, attempted aggravated murder, attempted arson, and assault in the second degree. This all stemmed from her involvement in hiring three men to kill her ex-boyfriend, Darren Cox.

Darren and Sarah had been in a relationship for three years. Darren had recently broken it off citing Sarah's increasingly bizarre behavior. After they broke up, Darren read a portion of her journal, wherein she wrote about wanting to burn his house down and trashing his car. This information put Darren on alert, which is how he ended up alive after not one, not two, but three attempts on his life.

Sarah was accused of hiring three hitmen to kill Darren. The hitmen were Michael Skipper, age twenty-three, Jesse Sanchez-Garcia, age twenty-three, and Michael Collicut, age twenty-six.

The first attempt on Darren's life was when his truck burst into flames. He was not inside the truck at the time. The next attempt was a drive-by shooting that occurred at his house before dawn. The third attempt was the closest he came to death.

Darren was at his house when he heard the doorbell ring. Due to his high alert status, he chose to look out the window instead of just opening the door. As Darren peered out the window, Jesse told Michael Skipper, that he saw Darren through the window. Michael immediately fired a shot through the window. Darren dove for cover while Jesse and Michael ran to the getaway car driven by Michael Collicut. The bullet hit Darren but he was able to immediately call the police.

With Michael Collicut at the wheel, the three hitmen managed to get away quickly from the crime scene. What the trio did not know was the police were watching the car because it had been reported stolen. The police attempted to stop the car, but Michael chose to elude the police. A police chase ensued but Michael's lack of driving skills proved he could not outrun the police. He ended up crashing the stolen car.

The three hitmen were arrested and charged with attempted aggravated murder, conspiracy to commit aggravated murder, and two counts of felony assault. Michael Collicut was also arrested on several warrants including; felony possession of a controlled substance, felony driving while revoked, felon in possession of a firearm, and attempting to elude the police. The trio ended up in different jails including Linn County, Yamhill County, and Benton County due to the crowded conditions at each jail.

Jesse told the investigators Sarah hired Michael Skipper, who he knew as "Fingers" to scare her ex-boyfriend. According to Jesse, Sarah paid Michael $1,000 to take care of Darren. Jesse claimed he was just along for the ride and had no idea there was a gun in the car, let alone that the car had been reported stolen.

In addressing Darren's three brushes with death, Benton County District Attorney Scott Heiser told reporters: "The only reason he wasn't killed was that he had the ability to recognize what was happening and dove for cover. Our expectation is that he would have been dead otherwise—we're fortunate we got them."[1]

Sarah's father put up 10 percent of her bail and she walked out of jail, but her time as a free woman was short lived. Four months after Sarah was freed from the county jail, the newspaper headlines read: "Woman arrested again for trying to arrange killing."

This time, Sarah allegedly tried to hire another hitman to finish the job the others failed at. The problem was this time, the hitman was an undercover cop. Sarah allegedly met the hitman in a parking lot in southeast Portland and made arrangements for him to take care of Darren once and for all. When the meeting was over, Sarah got back in her car and started to drive away. Police officers immediately turned on their lights and sirens, but Sarah took off at a high rate of speed. After a short police chase, she was taken into custody. Sarah was charged with attempted aggravated murder and solicitation to commit murder. Her attorney agreed to not ask to have her released on bail. "We're actually kind of unclear why she hated him this badly," said Benton County Deputy District Attorney Liane Richardson. Deputy District Attorney Richardson told the media they had been trying to assure Darren he was safe, but after this incident, it was harder to convince him of that.

Prior to Sarah's second arrest, Darren had been receiving threatening phone calls that he suspected Sarah was involved with. A hearing had been set for the following month and the district attorney planned to ask the judge to revoke her bail and place her back in jail. That hearing was cancelled after she was arrested for the second time.

Jesse pled guilty to attempted murder and attempted arson, after it was proven he was involved with two of the attempts on Darren's life. He was sentenced to nine years and three months in prison. Michael Collicut pled guilty to attempted murder. He received a sentence of seven years and six months in prison.

Michael Skipper pled guilty to attempted murder with a firearm. He was sentenced to seven years in prison. Benton County Circuit Judge Janet Holcomb addressed Michael saying, "It's hard to understand jeopardizing the lives of others for money, maybe a few hundred dollars. The court finds it hard to understand ... it's a very serious event and could have ruined several lives."[2]

The court gave Darren the opportunity to speak at Michael's sentencing. He showed photographs of two children who were in the house at the time he was shot. Speaking in a raised voice, he told Michael that he could have killed the children or his parents, who were also in the house at the time of the shooting. Darren told Michael he needed to get an education while in prison and become a productive member of society. Looking squarely at Michael, he said, "I hope that in jail you can find remorse. Dark clothes, nighttime and guns won't protect you where you're going."[3]

Sarah pled guilty to one count of attempted aggravated murder and one count of conspiracy to commit felony arson. She was found to be criminally insane on the arson charge. Sarah was sentenced to fourteen years in prison and three years of post-prison supervision. She was ordered to pay $11,760 in restitution.

Benton County Circuit Judge Ken Osher stipulated Sarah was to begin serving her sentence at the Oregon State Mental Hospital. He stated she was prohibited from attempting to persuade the Psychiatric Security Review Board, hospital staff, corrections staff, or any other Oregon authority to allow her to be treated or incarcerated anywhere other than a prison or state hospital in Oregon. Judge Osher made it clear that when Sarah finished her stint in the Oregon State Mental Hospital, she was to be physically moved to a prison in Oregon. He also stipulated she was not eligible for work release, any temporary leaves, a reduction in sentencing, or any alternative incarceration programs.

15
Charles Edwin Pease

The body of Charles Pease was located in a wooded area outside of Winston near Porter Creek and Highway 42 in September 1988. Detectives arrived and knew immediately they were dealing with a homicide. Charles' neck had been slashed and he had bled out where he had been left to die. Days earlier, his abandoned truck had been located nearby with his dogs still in the truck. A search began, leading to the discovery of his body.

The investigation into Charles' murder spanned several counties in Oregon and took half a year. In April 1988, the detectives wrapped up their investigation and prepared to bring in those responsible for the murder. Twelve law enforcement agencies served search warrants at nine locations spread out among four counties in Oregon. Ricky Leon Douglas, age thirty-one, was arrested and charged with aggravated murder. David Ray Marr, age twenty-seven, was also arrested and charged with aggravated murder.

The investigation revealed that Ricky allegedly paid David $10,000 to murder Charles who was living with Ricky's former wife. Ricky had married a young lady on a whirlwind trip to Reno six months prior. The relationship did not last. She filed for divorce and returned to Charles, her longtime boyfriend. The investigators believed David and a friend lured Charles to the remote forested area by promising him some marijuana if he would help them with a car that had broken down on a country road. Charles agreed to help and drove his own truck out to the area. Once Charles arrived, David allegedly came up behind him and used a hunting knife to cut his throat.

Law enforcement also uncovered that Ricky and David were major players in the methamphetamine manufacturing business in Oregon. During the execution of the search warrants, the police seized equipment and chemicals used to manufacture methamphetamine in mobile laboratories. They also seized half a pound of methamphetamine. They seized a house that belonged to Ricky, thought to have been purchased with proceeds from illegal drug sales. They also seized numerous vehicles, weapons, a marijuana-growing operation, and $20,000 in cash. At Ricky's house in Eugene, the police seized "high-tech surveillance equipment including cameras and devices used to detect wire taps in telephones and on people."

The police seized one methamphetamine manufacturing laboratory that they referred to it as a "highly sophisticated mobile methamphetamine laboratory." The police believed Ricky was making $500,000 a year manufacturing methamphetamine.

In referring to the seizures, Douglas County Sheriff's Office Undersheriff Ray Duncan told reporters, "We are going to hurt them any way we can—put them in jail, sure, but we're going to take away their profits too." He referred to their drug manufacturing operation as "widespread and hard core." Undersheriff Duncan said they had made "a big dent" in Oregon's methamphetamine business.

The detectives interviewed Ladd Dryan Justeson, age twenty-nine. He admitted to being involved with the murder. According to his taped statement to the police, David paid him $1,000 to assist him in killing Charles. He told the police he and David drove around Myrtle Creek for hours looking for Charles' car. When they saw it parked at a local grocery store, they made contact with Charles. They allegedly told him they needed help with a truck that had broken down on a remote road. They asked Charles to follow them to the remote area and if he helped them, they would share their marijuana with him. Ladd described how David used a large knife to slash Charles' throat. The police were never able to recover the weapon.

David was known to carry knives and had threatened a Coos County Sheriff's Office lieutenant with a knife two weeks prior to his arrest for Charles' murder. Lieutenant Bob Greene was at his own house when the altercation took place. David fled the scene after the altercation but was arrested the following day. A non-jury hearing was held before Circuit Court Judge High Downer. Lieutenant Greene testified that he was at home when David drove up his driveway on his motorcycle. He said David was agitated and demanded the return of a leather bag. It was Lieutenant Greene's testimony that David threatened to slice his throat if he attempted to take the knife away from David.

Lieutenant Greene admitted he ran back inside his house and retrieved his 9-mm service revolver. He said he went back outside, pointed the weapon at David, and told him he was under arrest. He testified that David took a step forward and he fired a round at David's feet. David, he said, got back on his motorcycle and took off at a high rate of speed. It was then, Lieutenant Greene said, that he fired four more rounds into the ground in the hopes it would scare David enough that he would not return. During the hearing, Lieutenant Greene told the court:

> At first I thought it was some bizarre kind of joke. He literally growled at me. With his posture and growling, I thought he was going to attack me. My intention was to put the fear of God into him. If he was going to leave, I wanted to make sure he wasn't going to come back.[1]

David's defense attorney, Mike Lehman, told the court that David never pulled out his knife. He accused Lieutenant Greene of being a less-than-credible witness who "overreacted to the situation."

David took the stand in his own defense and stated he arrived at Lieutenant Greene's house on friendly terms. He added that Lieutenant Greene never told him he was a police officer.

A review board at the Coos County Sheriff's Office did their own investigation into the incident. After reviewing the testimony of all involved, they concluded Lieutenant Greene was within his right to fire the first shot, but he was in violation of policy for firing the other four shots.

Circuit Court Judge Downer convicted David on menacing and sentenced him to eighteen months in jail. He also sentenced David to serve a concurrent one month in jail for a charge of trespassing. He felt the state had not proven that David ever intended to use the knife, therefore he did not impose a felony conviction for being in possession of a dangerous weapon with the intent to use it.

A year after David was arrested and charged with aggravated murder, his trial began in Douglas County. David was represented by defense attorneys, Leeon "Butch" Aller and Melvin "Bud" Smith. The state of Oregon was represented by Assistant Attorney General Doug Dawson. The jury was made up of seven women and five men.

The defense team filed a motion asking that their client be allowed to plead guilty to murder, just as Ladd had done. The prosecution argued that it was David who actually killed Charles. Assistant Attorney General Dawson explained that Ladd had only been an accessory to the murder, which is why he was allowed to plead to a lesser sentence. Judge Thomas W. Kolberg denied the defense motion.

Ladd was called to the stand to testify against David. He had agreed to do so in exchange for escaping a possible death sentence. In his plea bargain, he was allowed to plead guilty to a charge of murder instead of aggravated murder that could have resulted in the death penalty.

Ladd said he and David injected methamphetamine the night before the murder. He said he and David both had girlfriends. He added that David and his girlfriend had four children. Ladd said they all lived together in a house in Coos Bay. He mentioned that the girlfriends were sisters.

Ladd explained that he and David were planning on going into the methamphetamine manufacturing business together. Their plans fell through, he said, when they were unable to break into a community college to steal glassware.

Ladd told the court he and David lured Charles to a remote spot out in the woods with the promise of sharing their marijuana with him. Ladd testified he was 20 feet away from David when he saw David come up behind Charles and slash his throat.

Ladd said, "Mr. Pease looked at me and said, 'help me.' Mr. Marr guided him to the ground." Ladd testified that once they were back in David's truck leaving the scene of the crime, David allegedly said, "Do you think I cut him good enough."

Ladd also told the jurors on the drive home that David asked him to feel his chest. He explained, "He asked me to put my hand on his heart to see that it wasn't beating at an abnormal rate. For some reason, he wanted to assure me he wasn't upset with what he had done." Ladd testified he wiped the knife clean and disposed of it in a stream. He said they then drove home to Coos Bay.

David's girlfriend testified against him. She told the court she had disposed of some bloody clothes at his request. She also stated David had told her he killed Charles. David took the witness stand and explained that even though he agreed to murder Charles, he never intended to go through with the plan. He admitted to accepting a down payment from Ricky, that consisted of cash and drugs. It was David's testimony that Ladd was the one who murdered Charles.

The jury deliberated for nearly six hours before announcing they had reached a verdict. Just before midnight, on March 22, 1989, David learned he had been found guilty of aggravated murder. Two weeks later, the same jury returned to the courtroom to decide whether or not to impose the death penalty. Prior to beginning deliberations, each side had one more chance to convince the jurors of David's innocence or guilt.

Forensic psychologist John Cochran testified on behalf of the prosecution. In describing David's behavior, he said, "He is detached from others. He is not able to empathize. He has no shame, guilt or remorse." He went onto say David had an anti-social personality and would never be able to overcome that. Psychologist Clifford Custer was called by the defense team. Clifford blamed David's problems on his mother's near death from a motorcycle accident and his alcoholic father. Clifford emphatically told the jury, "I hold hope out for David."

In his closing remarks, Assistant Attorney General Dawson reminded the jurors that David refused to take the blame for killing Charles. He told the jurors, "This is a man who is so cold he can kill somebody he doesn't know for money." He referred to David as a cold-blooded killer and asked the jury to sentence David to death. Leeon addressed the jury by saying:

> Thirty years from now, I hope you will be asking yourself, "I wonder if David Marr took advantage of the chance we gave him?" I hope you're not asking yourself, "I wonder if he would have taken advantage if we'd given him the chance?"

Looking at each juror, Leeon reminded them that the only time his client had been in trouble with the law, was when he was doing drugs. In conclusion he stated, "There's no doubt that David Marr is a tragedy. But he's fixable. He can be made to be human again."

It took the jury eight hours to decide if David should be sentenced to death. In the end, they returned a life imprisonment sentence with a mandatory minimum of thirty years. David embraced his attorneys before being led away by jail deputies to begin a life behind bars.

Melvin told the waiting reporters, "I think the jury reached the verdict that it was obvious David Marr is not the worst of the worst. I think the death penalty should be reserved for the worst of the worst."

David received an additional six months for assaulting a fellow inmate at the prison. He was charged with assault and possession of a weapon after stabbing an inmate in the face using a homemade knife. He pled guilty to assault.

It took longer to select a jury in Ricky's trial than it took to hold the trial. Douglas County Deputy District Attorney Bill Marshall told the jury the state's case would sound like a low-grade movie. He explained, "But we're stuck with a plot the defendant gave us in this case." Ricky's defense attorney, Bill Marshall, argued the case was based on circumstantial evidence. He told the jury there was nothing to link his client to the actual crime. He suggested David killed Charles and then blackmailed Ricky.

After listening to the evidence, the jury filed out to begin deliberations. After several hours, they returned to the courtroom with a verdict of guilty of aggravated murder. Two weeks later, the same jury was back in the deliberation room, this time to decide whether to sentence Ricky to death or life imprisonment. The questions put before them were: Whether Ricky acted deliberately in hiring the killer; whether Ricky would pose a threat to society in the future; and whether Ricky acted unreasonably to any provocation there may have been. Despite the defense's pleas for mercy, the jury returned a verdict of a death sentence. Ricky's defense attorney promised he would appeal the sentence.

Two years after Ricky was sentenced to die for the murder of Charles, the Oregon Supreme Court reviewed his case. At issue was the defense's claim that Ricky was not allowed to enter into evidence a rebuttal to the prosecution's attack on his character. The Oregon Supreme Court upheld Ricky's conviction of aggravated murder but they overturned his death sentence. A new trial was ordered to reevaluate his sentence.

Ricky's second trial had barely begun, when a juror told the judge she no longer believed she could be impartial. The juror was dismissed from her civic duty. The trial proceeded with an alternate juror. After two days of deliberations, they returned a sentence of life in prison with a mandatory thirty years, thus freeing Ricky from death row.

16

Hitman For Hire

Shane Sichting was living in Libby, Montana, when he decided he needed to hire a hitman to kill his wife. Shane owned the American Muscle Autoworks in Libby. He spoke to his employee, Ronald Morales, about the possibility of hiring a hitman. Ronald agreed to help Shane find a hitman. He accepted $30,000 as a down payment for his work. The agreed-upon price was $50,000, but instead of trying to find a hitman, Ronald took the $30,000 and returned to his family home in Eugene.

From time to time, Shane would phone Ronald to check on his progress in finding a hitman. He continued to send money to Ronald as per their agreement. Ronald eventually received the entire $50,000. He was still living in Eugene and had no plans to return to Montana, let alone hire a hitman to murder Shane's wife. Once the last of the money arrived, he stopped communicating with Shane, figuring the situation would just go away when Shane realized he had been scammed. Ronald explained the money to his family by saying he had won the lottery.

When Shane showed up on Ronald's doorstep in Eugene, Ronald panicked. It was then he knew he needed to contact the police. Ronald explained to the police what had happened and that Shane was now in Eugene, expecting Ronald to hire a hitman using the $50,000 he had paid. With the help of the police, Ronald put into motion a ploy to make Shane believe he had hired a hitman who was in Montana. Shane left Eugene and headed back to Libby.

Once in Libby, arrangements were made for Shane to meet with the hitman. An undercover officer from the Kalispell Police Department met with Shane. He told Shane he had been paid $50,000 and was ready to carry out the hit on Shane's wife. He asked Shane how he wanted the murder done. In an effort to prove his credentials, he explained to Shane that his usual mode of operation was to make it look like a carjacking. He described how he would shoot her in the head and steal her purse to make it look authentic.

The two men talked at length and made the necessary arrangements. As they left the meeting, other officers swooped in and arrested Shane. He was charged with a federal crime of using Interstate commerce in the commission of murder for hire. Shane pled not guilty in federal court before U.S. Magistrate Judge Jeremiah Lynch. Two months later, a trial was held in federal court.

Chief U.S. District Judge Don Molloy was the presiding judge. Assistant U.S. Attorney Kris McLean was the prosecutor. John Rhodes was the federal defender. The jury consisted of six women and six men.

Assistant U.S. Attorney McLean opened by saying, "This case is about the defendant hiring a hit man to kill his wife." John opened by explaining the money given to Ronald was to purchase his truck, not to hire a hitman. He explained that Ronald's testimony should not be trusted, in as much as he had only agreed to cooperate with law enforcement after being granted immunity for his part in the case. He went onto say Ronald had a lengthy criminal record and was known to abuse illegal drugs.

During the trial, a recorded conversation was played wherein Shane allegedly was heard saying he still wanted the "motor fixed." The prosecution contended this meant he still wanted his wife killed. Shane had told the F.B.I. agents after his arrest that what he was referring to was sabotaging his wife's car so she could not take the children and leave town. "I thought we were talking about putting Tootsie Rolls in her gas tank," Shane told the F.B.I. agents.

Yet Ronald said when he asked "for a picture of the motor," Shane sent him a photograph of his wife. He also allegedly sent Ronald directions through MapQuest to the house his wife was staying at. All eyes were on Shane's wife, Sheilagh, when she took the witness stand. She told of enduring abuse at the hands of Shane. She said she filed for divorce because she had become increasingly afraid of him. She spoke of financial difficulties over the years. Sheilagh told the court Shane had become extremely angry over losing custody of their two young children.

A young lady who had been in a romantic relationship with Shane took the witness stand. She told the court they had a relationship while Shane was in the midst of his divorce. It was her testimony that Shane continually spoke of "taking out" his wife.

In recorded telephone calls from the jail where Shane was housed following his arrest, he allegedly spoke to his girlfriend on the phone. In one telephone conversation, Shane allegedly admitted to paying Ronald $5,000 to kill his wife. During the call, he accused his wife of stealing money from his business. Shane allegedly said, "As far as I'm concerned, she doesn't even deserve to suck air."

The jury watched the videotaped interview that the F.B.I. agents conducted with Shane following his arrest. In the interview, he admitted to paying Ronald to hire a hitman, but explained he quickly changed his mind and got part of the money back. Shane explained to the agents:

> Anybody who's been divorced, it's gone through their mind. Yeah, it went through my mind. But I didn't decide overnight. I mean, we're talking about the mother of my children. I thought about it for four or five days.

After three hours of deliberations, the jury returned a verdict of guilty of using interstate communication to commit murder for hire. They based this on a wire transfer Shane sent to Ronald's bank account in Oregon. U.S. District Judge Molloy sentenced Shane to the maximum term of ten years in federal prison and three years of post-prison supervision. The following year, Shane's appeal was turned down by a panel of three appellate judges, but this would not be the last time the courts heard from Shane.

Shane was nearing the end of his ten-year prison sentence when he made yet another attempt to hire a hitman. Having not yet given up on having his now ex-wife murdered, he decided to give it another try. This time though, in addition to having Sheilagh killed, he also wanted to hire a hitman to kill Ronald.

Shane allegedly approached a fellow inmate with his request. The inmate went along with the plot but was actually informing the authorities at the same time. The inmate provided Shane with a phone number of a hitman. The "hitman" was actually an F.B.I. agent. A total of four calls were allegedly made between Shane and the "hitman." They agreed on a price of $10,000 for each murder.

Shane was arrested and charged with using interstate commerce in the commission of murder and retaliating against an informant. During an interview with F.B.I. agents, Shane waived his rights to an attorney and wrote out a confession that totaled nine pages.

At a court hearing, the defense moved that neither the interview nor the confession be allowed into evidence. The judge denied the motion and Shane pled guilty to both charges. Shane was sentenced to eleven years in federal prison. He was forty-eight years old at the time he began his second sentence.

17
The Goggins

"I finally figured if he's going to kill me, he's going to kill me, and I can't just stand here and let it happen." Bobby Wilson recalled her ordeal when the hitman her husband hired to kill her came at her. Bobby explained to the jury the hitman attempted to strangle her with a wire backpacker's saw and inflicted numerous cuts during the struggle. She managed to get away, thus ruining her husband's chance at cashing in on her $100,000 life insurance policy. Robert Leslie Goggin was sentenced to seventeen years in prison.

During Robert's trial, the would-be hitman took the witness stand and admitted he had read a book on how to be a successful hitman. After the trial, Bobby sued the publishing house that published the book, *Hit Man: A Technical Manual for Independent Contractors*. It was not the first time the publishing house had been sued regarding the book. In her lawsuit, Bobby outlined two dozen tips that were listed in the book that she believed the hitman hired to kill her used as a guide. Bobby settled out of court with the publishing house.

18
David G. Bennett

On the night of November 9, 1985, police rushed to a call of a stabbing in Laurelhurst Park in Portland. When they arrived, they found David Bennett, age forty-five, with multiple stab wounds. David died a short time later at Providence Medical Center.

David's wife, Deloris, age forty-five, was with him at the park, as was a friend, Ernest Raymond Martinez, age thirty-three. Deloris and Ernest told the police the three of them decided to take a walk about 11 p.m. because they wanted to see if the ducks were still in the pond at the park. Both Deloris and Ernest said as they were walking in the park, a man suddenly jumped from behind a bush and stabbed David. Deloris told the investigators, "I heard my husband scream and say, 'Oh, my God!' Then Diablo [Ernest] pushed me out of the way and told me to run and get some help."[1] Deloris explained that she ran to a nearby gas station and called the police.

Ernest told the police the assailant attacked him when he tried to help David. "He just jumped out of the bushes when we walked by and he didn't say a thing. Dave and him fell to the ground before I knew what was going on. Dave was short and was not a fighter. He wasn't strong. I went to help Dave and I got kicked in the groin and was hit in the face."[2] Ernest added that his glasses were knocked from his face during the attack so he was unable to get a good look at the assailant.

Deloris told the investigators her husband was an audit clerk at the Pacific Power and Light Company. She said they regularly opened their home to those in need. She said Ernest was a drifter and was homeless so they allowed him to move in with them. "Our belief was that God put us here to help others. We don't have a lot to offer, but what we do, we will share with others."[3]

Once news of the stabbing hit the newspapers and local news, the public became very concerned. Portland Police Homicide Detective Tom Nelson told the media they did not have any suspects in the unprovoked stabbing.

From the start, things did not add up for the detectives working the case. Within two weeks of David's murder, Deloris and Ernest found themselves in handcuffs being transported to jail. Another friend of Deloris', Ray Dean Clark, age nineteen, joined them in jail. The three were charged with conspiracy to commit murder. They were held without bail. Portland Police Sergeant Jay Decker told the media, "Clark and Martinez were street people that the Bennetts had taken in and all three conspired to kill him."

A jury consisting of ten women and two men heard the case against Ernest. Ernest's defense attorney, Bradley Grove, told the jury Ernest had had a terrible childhood. He allegedly had endured physical and sexual abuse as a child. Bradley explained when Ernest heard allegations of child abuse by David, he decided to take matters into his own hands.

After nearly five hours of deliberations, they returned a verdict of guilty of two counts of aggravated murder. Ernest was also convicted on the charge of aiding and abetting Ray and convicted of hiring Ray to commit the murder. When the verdict was read out loud in the courtroom, Ernest began crying and had to be restrained by security guards.

The same jury returned a week later to decide if Ernest should be sentenced to death. In the end, the vote was not unanimous for the death penalty. The sticking point was the probability that Ernest would commit future acts of violence constituting a continuing threat to society. Multnomah County Circuit Judge Robert P. Jones sentenced Ernest to life in prison with a minimum of thirty years. Ernest began crying and held his head in his hands when the verdict was announced.

Ray Clark was convicted and sentenced to life in prison. As part of a plea agreement, he did not receive the death penalty.

Deloris also received a sentence of life in prison. Seven years after entering the woman's prison, Deloris was interviewed by the *Statesman Journal*. The newspaper was doing an article about a new program in the prison called "Abused Living Females." The group was for women who had either killed their husband or partner or attempted to do so. She told reporter Sarah Peamine, "I get really angry at myself because I still love my husband. I would stay in here for the rest of my life if I thought I could bring my husband back." Deloris recalled telling her attorney that she would accept the death penalty if it could be done quickly. During her trial she thought, "What if the jury acquits me? I deserve to be punished."[4]

19
John Lucas

On November 10, 1987, John Robert Lucas' family filed a missing person report after he failed to return home after a business meeting. His wife and five sons began an intensive search. The family hired a helicopter and from the air, they spotted John's truck. Two days after he was last seen alive, John's body was discovered on an old logging road east of Scio, about 8 miles southwest of Lyons. John had been shot in the head.

John, who was forty-six years old at the time of his death, had lived in Stayton his entire life. For many years, he owned John Lucas Chevrolet in Stayton. He was a co-owner of Lucas Homes Incorporated along with his wife, Kathy, and his son, Michael.

To complicate things even more, the police learned three people working together had tried to scam $20,000 from John's son, Michael, who had received a phone call from a man who claimed he had documents relating to his father's death. The man asked Michael to meet him at a parking lot on Mission Street in Salem. He told Michael he would give him the documents in exchange for $20,000. Michael agreed to meet the man, but he immediately notified Linn County Sheriff's Office.

The meeting was arranged for a Sunday at noon. Standing by in the background were two detectives with the Linn County Sheriff's Office, detectives with the Salem Police Department's Selective Investigations Unit, and Special Agents with the F.B.I.

Michael met with the man at the arranged time. Law enforcement furnished him with $5,000 to use as a down payment. Once Michael gave the money to the man, law enforcement made an arrest. The man was identified as Roger Jay Ringgenberg, age twenty-five. He told the detectives he was a middleman for the person who had the documents relating to his father's death. A short time later, Brian Wayne McClellan, age thirty-two, and Cari Lynn Fiske, age twenty-four, were arrested. All three people were charged with theft by extortion and conspiracy to commit aggravated theft. Marion County Deputy District Attorney Kirk Engdall explained:

> At this point in time, it looks like an attempt by the suspects to extort members of the Lucas family. It appears to just be a scam to try and get some bucks. At this point, what we have is an arrest for an attempted theft, and I don't anticipate anything more than that.

He told the reporters he did not believe the trio had anything to do with the murder. Reporter Marilyn Montgomery with the *Albany Democrat-Herald* asked Linn County Sheriff's Office Detective Lieutenant Dar Holm about the documents. He said there was no transfer of documents at the meeting and the $5,000 was recovered. In describing what the documents were supposed to be, he said, "He gave a brief description of it; he was really vague. He said it was on some letterhead stationery, something like a list of the steps leading up to the murder." Roger and Brian pled guilty to a charge of criminal conspiracy. Cari received a suspended sentence and was fined $300 and placed on two years' probation.

Early in the homicide investigation, a person of interest was identified as Chris Lange, age forty. The detectives working the case were anxious to talk to Chris about his possible involvement in the murder. However, Chris was in a jail in Columbus, Georgia, on a menacing charge. He had only been in Georgia a short time. His third wife and child lived in Georgia, as did his previous wives and two children. He went back and forth between the states on a regular basis. In Oregon, he was using the name Stephen Rex Barrett. He had his name legally changed to Chris Soren Lange. He also used the alias of Darrel Dow.

Detectives with the Linn County Sheriff's Office traveled to Georgia twice to interview Chris. He was not charged with any crime involving John's death. When Chris failed to appear on some criminal charges he had pending in Oregon, a warrant was issued for his arrest. The detectives were able to have Chris extradited from Georgia. They flew out to Georgia and brought Chris back to Oregon.

Chris had charges pending in three counties—Wheeler, Marion, and Linn. His bail was originally set at $20,000. He tried to post bond, but Judge James Gleeson raised the bail to $250,000. Linn County Sheriff Art Martinak said: "He didn't appear before when he was allowed to remain free on a lesser amount, and this was the second time he'd gone to Georgia. The court apparently thinks he's not a good risk."

Chris' first appearance was in Linn County on a charge of making a false application for a license and driving under the influence of intoxicants. Chris pled innocent to the driving charge but wanted to wait for an attorney to answer to the license charge. His next appearance was for a theft charge, also in Linn County. That case involved the theft of a typewriter the police found in his car that matched the description of a typewriter that had been stolen from an office at a lumber mill. Chris had a warrant out of Marion County for possession of cocaine. His warrant out of Wheeler County was for a parole violation.

Once Chris was back in Oregon, the detectives with the Linn County Sheriff's Office interviewed him again in regards to John's death but they did not arrest him. Chris was able to post bond a week later. Chris failed to appear as agreed when he posted bail.

The Oregon State Police placed Chris on the top ten fugitive list. Under his physical description, they wrote, "At one time he was ranked high as a heavyweight professional boxer. He has a violent temper and is prone to violence." They listed his prior convictions as burglary, car theft, possession of cocaine, felony driving with a suspended driver's license, and failure to appear in court. The authorities learned Chris was back in Georgia. Once again, he was extradited to Oregon. This time he was accompanied by Detective P. J. Miller and Deputy Dale White of the Linn County Sheriff's Office.

When Chris was arrested in Georgia, he was in possession of several guns that he was prohibited from owning due to his previous felony convictions. Once he was back in Oregon, he appeared in a federal court in Eugene on a federal charge of being a felon in possession of a weapon. Chris pled guilty and was sentenced to fourteen months in a federal prison. He requested to be placed in a federal prison near his wife and child in Georgia.

The investigation into John's murder continued. Nearly one year after he was killed, his wallet was found by a hunter; it was located on the bank of the Santiam River, about 6 miles from where his body was found. John's credit cards were in the wallet but his driver's license and business cards were missing.

Detective Lieutenant Holm sent divers into the river in search of the missing items but they came up empty-handed. The divers had been out on five separate occasions trying to locate the murder weapon. Additionally, the Linn County Sheriff's Office explorer search and rescue post had searched through brush on three separate occasions and did not have any success.

Just over eighteen months after John's body was discovered, the Linn County grand jury returned a secret indictment against three men for the murder of John Lucas. David Virgil Waldner, age forty-two, was arrested and charged with aggravated murder and murder. The investigators believed David hired Chris Lange and Donald Dow, age forty-two, to murder John. They believed Chris was the one who shot John in the head. Their investigation led them to believe that the homicide had been planned up to two months prior to when John was killed. Donald and Chris were charged with aggravated murder and murder. Chris was serving time in a federal prison in Memphis, Tennessee, when he was charged with John's murder. The authorities in Oregon filed documents to extradite Chris back to Oregon.

David had worked as the manager of the used car division at John's car dealership four years before his death. After leaving there, he established his own wholesale car business. Donald owned a carwash business.

Months before this arrest, Donald pled guilty to a federal charge of selling firearms to a felon; the felon who purchased the weapons was Chris. The sale took place a few months before John was murdered. A total of three weapons changed hands. Donald's sentence was suspended and he was placed on probation for three years.

Donald pled guilty to two counts of hindering prosecution for his role in John's murder. All other charges were dropped when he agreed to testify against David and Chris. One of the charges of hindering the prosecution was not telling the investigators he had picked up an envelope containing money from David and given it to Chris. The other hindering prosecution charge was due to Donald providing Chris with his late brother Darrel's birth certificate so that Chris could use it as an alias. Donald was placed on probation for five years and ordered to serve one week in jail. He was also ordered to pay $1,000 in fines and reimburse the county for his legal fees, estimated at $1,000.

David's defense attorney, Kenneth Morrow requested that his client be allowed to post bail. A bail hearing was held before Linn County Circuit Court Judge William O. Lewis. Judge Lewis asked the reporters to restrict what they put in their newspapers, saying he was concerned about being able to seat an impartial jury, if the public read too many details of what would be discussed at the bail hearing. Judge Lewis warned each newspaper reporter that if he did not have their cooperation, he might have to close the bail hearing to the reporters. The *Statesman Journal* consulted with their attorney who deemed it within their First Amendment right to report everything that happened at the bail hearing. The judge agreed and the bail hearing continued.

A total of eighteen witnesses took the stand to testify during the bail hearing. Donald was one of the witnesses. He told the court he had known both David and Chris for fifteen years. He said one day, David "asked me if I knew any shady characters who would do almost anything." He said Chris had worked for him from time to time. Then in a nonchalant manner that shocked everyone in the courtroom, Donald said David had hired Chris to commit arson by burning down his auto business in March 1987. Donald went onto say, "Lange told me Dave wanted to hire him to kill John Lucas."

On cross examination, Kenneth asked why Donald never reported this to the police. Donald said he did not think Chris would actually kill John. He then admitted that on November 10, 1987, Chris came to Donald's carwash in the late afternoon and announced that he had just killed John using a .22 caliber pistol that he had thrown in the river. Donald told the court that Chris had blood on his pants. He also said Chris told him he used John's truck to go over the tracks that his own truck made on the logging road. He then wiped his fingerprints from John's truck. You could hear a pin drop in the courtroom as Donald continued his testimony. He said Chris showed him John's car keys and wallet, adding that he stole the items at David's suggestion, so that it would look like a robbery.

Donald said he asked Chris if David was aware of what had just happened. It was Donald's testimony that Chris told him that he had stopped by a tavern and told David that he had just killed John. Donald said he later went to see David and picked up an envelope with an unknown amount of cash and gave it to Chris.

Linn County Deputy District Attorney George Eder took the witness stand and told the court that Chris had a telephone credit card. He then presented a record of all the telephone calls Chris had made, including one made from the tavern on the afternoon of the murder. Chris, he said, had also phoned David several times prior to the murder.

Kenneth argued the reason Chris had called David was because he was interested in purchasing a car from him.

An insurance agent, Ed Cravinho, testified that David and John had life insurance policies from the time they worked together. He explained they each took out a $75,000 double-indemnity policy on each other in 1984. The reason for this, he said, was because David had loaned John $75,000. After John's death, David collected $150,000 on the life insurance policy. This was based on the fact John did not die from natural causes, so the payout was double the amount of the life insurance policy.

Linn County Sheriff's Office Detective Paul Miller, who had worked the case from the beginning, told the court David told him he loaned John approximately $100,000, of which $45,000 had been repaid.

Kenneth argued the case against his client was circumstantial, saying, "Any one of those circumstances is capable of being disclaimed." He explained to Judge Lewis that David needed to operate his business in order to support his family. He reminded the court, "His ties to the community are significant. He has lived all his life in Salem. He has parents, grandparents, aunts, uncles, sisters, two kids, and a stepson. His daughter attends Oregon State University." He added that David did not have any criminal convictions. He told Judge Lewis, "Also, much of the money Mr. Waldner loaned to Mr. Lucas is still outstanding." He said David's money was tied up in constructing a new car business.[1]

Deputy District Attorney Eder argued the amount should be $1.5 million. He told Judge Lewis that not only did David have equity in his house, he had also collected $150,000 from the life insurance policy. Judge Lewis took the case under advisement. Days later, he set David's bail at $500,000. David posted the required 10 percent and walked out of jail.

Chris was extradited from the federal prison in Memphis, Tennessee. He pled innocent and was held without bail in the Linn County jail. The court appointed William Lyons to represent him. Weeks later, he requested a new attorney, citing that William was too busy to assist him.

A hearing was held to determine if David and Chris' trials should be consolidated or held separately. Deputy District Attorney Eder argued in favor of one trial for both defendants. Kenneth argued that the trials should be separated. After taking this request under advisement, Judge Lewis ruled that the trials would be held separately.

David's trial got underway. Linn County Deputy District Attorney George Eder represented the state of Oregon. Kenneth Morrow was the defense attorney. David took the witness stand in his own defense. Kenneth asked him, "Did you ever desire or request that John Lucas be dead?" To this, David quickly replied, "no!"

David told the jury that the life insurance policy that he had on John had lapsed. He did say that the day John's body was found, his insurance agent phoned him and told him he needed to pay the premium or else the policy would expire the following day. David told the court he did make the payment, but "I didn't feel right about it."

David described his relationship with John and the business, indicating that everything was fine in the beginning. "He was always really fair with me—at that point. Later it changed." He then spoke of the financial problems that plagued the business. He said he put $20,000 into the business and then borrowed $80,000 from banks to keep the business afloat. "There was always an overdraft at the bank." David said he had to be a guarantor for the company that financed their new General Motors cars because they deemed John too much of a financial risk.

David told the jury he left John's business to start his own wholesale car company. He said when he had his own business, he and John still did business together from time to time. Based on Donald's earlier testimony at the bail hearing, Kenneth asked David about the fire that swept through his business. "Did you ask anyone or cause anyone to set that place on fire?" The answer came quickly, "No way." Kenneth then asked, "Did you ask Donny Dow to find you someone shady? David simply said, "No."

"I knew I was innocent. I felt confident all along," exclaimed David after the jury acquitted him. David's family and friends began crying with relief. His parents, grandmother, wife, aunts, uncles, daughter, and friends were all present. Even though Judge Lewis asked them before the verdict was read to refrain from showing any emotion, they were unable to abide by the judge's request. When asked what his future plans were, David replied, "to just try and get it back together." David added, "I want it said that John Lucas was a dear friend of mine. This whole thing is crazy."

Prior to Chris' trial, the prosecution dropped the aggravated murder charge against him but kept the murder charge. They reasoned that since David was acquitted of hiring Chris, the aggravated murder charge was no longer relevant.

Linn County Circuit Judge Robert Gardner presided over Chris' trial. Chris was defended by attorneys Ralph Monson and Griffith Steinke. The prosecutor was Deputy District Attorney George Eder. The jury was made up of seven men and five women.

During Chris' trial, two inmates testified that Chris told them he had killed John. One of the inmates recalled Chris telling him John was a Chevrolet dealer and he had shot him once in the head. This confession allegedly happened while Chris was serving time in a federal prison. The defense questioned both inmates as to what they were trying to get out of the deal, for testifying. He also asked them to explain why they were in federal prison. One of the inmates admitted to being in federal prison for fraud and the other for bank robbery.

Ralph called Linn County Deputy District Attorney Eder to the witness stand. He asked him if either of the inmates who testified had received preferential treatment for their testimony. Deputy District Attorney Eder answered that one had requested a transfer to another federal prison. The other asked that the prison officials be told he was here as a defendant, not as a witness, to avoid being called a snitch within the prison. Deputy District Attorney Eder denied that either request had been granted. Judge Gardner asked the prosecutor if he wanted to cross examine his own self, to which he replied in the negative.

Donald took the stand and told the jury that he contacted Chris about possibly setting David's business on fire after David asked him to find "a shady character." Donald told the jury Chris told him details about the fire. Chris' attorney questioned Donald's veracity, saying he had changed his story several times when speaking to the detectives. The defense called several people to the stand, all of whom testified that Donald was a prolific liar.

The bookkeeper who worked for John testified that a man by the name of Bob Nolan called the business every day for two weeks prior to her boss' death. She said John spoke to the caller the morning he disappeared. She testified that he left the office within fifteen minutes of taking the phone call. She said he took brochures with him relating to his mobile home business when he left.

The prosecution presented phone bills from Chris' mother's phone that showed phone calls to John's business placed between September 29 to November 10. The phone bills also showed ten calls from Chris' mother's phone to David between October 26 and December 3. They noted a phone call to David at 1:22 p.m. on November 10.

The timing of the phone calls became a sticking point for both sides. The defense admitted Chris phoned John's office at 11:14 a.m. on the day he went missing, November 10. Chris claimed he was simply trying to set up a drug deal but he never spoke to John.

The prosecution stated the last phone call placed to John's business was on the day he disappeared at 11:14 a.m. Deputy District Attorney Eder told the jury:

> He's calling a lot of people on the 11th and 12th. Who doesn't he call? John Lucas, the man he was supposedly trying to make a drug deal with. It's no longer important, because it's no longer going to happen. The meeting is done. John Lucas is dead. He knows because he did it.[2]

David took the witness stand to testify against Chris. He told the jury he had known Chris for nine years, and during that time, he had frequently given him money. Ralph asked David if he ever hired Chris or anyone else to kill John. David quickly replied he had not. Ralph asked if he had ever hired Chris to kill anyone, to which David replied in the negative.

After the closing arguments, Ralph asked the judge to acquit Chris due to the fact "there simply is no credible evidence." Judge Gardner denied the request saying the case needed to be decided by a jury. With that, he gave instructions to the jury and sent them off to decide Chris' fate.

It took the jury less than one hour to return a verdict of guilty of murder. Judge Gardner sentenced Chris to life in prison with a minimum of twenty-five years before being eligible for parole, work release, temporary leave, or work camp. Judge Gardner referred to Chris as a "potentially very dangerous person."

A week after being acquitted, David was charged with arson. This stemmed from Donald's testimony regarding David allegedly hiring Chris to burn down his business. He allegedly paid Chris $5,000 and gave him a gun for committing the arson. Kenneth Morrow represented him on the new charge. He told the jury that David did not have anything to do with the fire that destroyed his wholesale automobile company in March 1987. He was also facing a charge of theft relating to a payment he received from the insurance company that should have been turned over to the lienholder.

It was decided that in this case, David and Chris would be tried together. Deputy District Stephen Dingle represented the state. Chris was represented by Griffith Steinke. Both men pled innocent to three counts of criminal conspiracy, two counts of arson, and one count of reckless burning.

Kenneth argued there was no motive to set the business on fire because it was underinsured. Griffith told the jury Donald's testimony was not credible, citing his many versions of what supposedly happened. The jury acquitted both men on all charges.

After the acquittal, Kenneth explained to reporters for the *Stateman Journal,* "Motive doesn't exist. He didn't profit from this fire." He went onto say the business was underinsured. He explained David received $20,000 for the building and $19,900 for a classic Jensen-Healey that was worth $35,000, but he did not receive anything for the contents of the business.

Eleven years into his prison sentence, Chris was asked by the *Statesman Journa*l about the boxing program in prison. Chris had a background in boxing prior to going to prison. Chris told the media:

A lot of these guys were raised tough in the first place, so they like to see this kind of contact. Believe it or not, it helps them relieve stress and keeps them out of trouble in the yard. They can release it right here.

Shortly before Chris was eligible for parole, he was killed in the prison yard. Prison officials told the media Chris was beaten to death during a brawl at the Snake River Correctional Institution.

20
Robert Eugene Harris

Robert finished his graveyard shift at Rosboro Lumber Company in Springfield and headed out to the parking lot. He got into his Ford Fiesta and prepared to drive home. As he turned the key, a huge explosion ripped through the car. The doors were blown off the car, as was part of the roof. Robert's coworkers found him lying near the driver's side of the car and described his clothing as "pretty much shredded." They called emergency services and Robert was rushed to the McKenzie-Willamette Hospital. Eleven hours later, Robert died from his injuries. The cause of Robert's death was "massive hemorrhage and tissue destruction as a result of the blast."

Police interviewed Robert's coworkers and his family. His wife, Barbara, did tell the investigators that their seventeen-year-old daughter's boyfriend had threatened Robert. She could not recall how long ago that happened or what was said. Otherwise, the police had very little to go on. The U.S. Bureau of Alcohol, Tobacco and Firearms (ATF) were called in to analyze the evidence left behind.

Two weeks after the bombing, Springfield Police Department Lieutenant Leroy Bergstrom said they were "making progress" in their investigation. "We've got a lot of leads. We're satisfied with the direction we're going." They interviewed the man Barbara had mentioned.

The Lumber and Sawmill Workers Union that Robert belonged to offered a $1,000 reward for information leading to the arrest and conviction of the person(s) responsible. Barbara received $12,000 in life insurance proceeds. Additionally, every employee at the Rosboro Lumber Company where Robert had worked for seventeen years donated money to Barbara, which amounted to several hundred dollars.

Six weeks after the car bomb killed Robert, his wife was arrested and charged with aggravated murder and murder. Terry James White, age thirty-two, was also taken into custody and charged with the same crimes. Lieutenant Bergstrom told the media the arrests came about after "long, hard, tedious work. We eventually developed sufficient cause to effect an arrest. We just never gave up on it. There were several directions we were going in, and this is one of them." Part of their investigation led them to Terry when they learned the Harris' seventeen-year-old daughter was living with Terry. Both Barbara and Terry pled innocent.

Michael Kell, age nineteen, was the final person to be arrested. The police located him in California and brought him back to Oregon. He was also charged with murder. Michael pled innocent to the charges against him.

The three defendants were tried separately. Michael was the first of the trio to be tried. During his trial, he admitted to stealing the dynamite used in the bombing from the Christian Logging Company in Springfield. He said he drove Terry to the parking lot of the mill where Robert worked but was never involved in any discussions about killing Robert. When he was asked if he felt any responsibility for what happened, he replied, "I suppose if the dynamite had never been stolen, it would never have happened." He admitted he felt responsible and he regretted giving any technical advice to Terry.

A fellow inmate of Michael's took the stand and told the jury that Michael confessed the crime to him while they were playing cards. He said Michael told him he took part in the murder "because of what Mr. Harris did to his daughter." He informed the jury that Michael told him he went with Terry and Barbara and visited Robert's workplace that night "to make sure the car was parked in the right place." To counter that testimony, the defense called an inmate to the stand who said Michael never talked about what he was locked up for.

In his closing remarks, Lane County District Attorney Brian Barnes referred to the crime as "a cold-blooded assassination." He stressed that this was premeditated with great detail to the plan. "Quite frankly, the state views this as a case of finding [Michael] guilty of aggravated murder or of nothing. It is an all or nothing case. He asked the jury to not "plea bargain the case in the jury room."[1]

On the defense side, Michael Phillips claimed Michael was naïve, but not guilty of committing murder. The jury felt otherwise and returned a guilty verdict. Lane County Circuit Court Judge Douglas Spencer told the jury they could find Michael guilty of aggravated murder, manslaughter, or criminally negligent homicide. They chose aggravated murder. After the verdict, Judge Spencer told the media, "I thought the verdict of the jury in this case was the proper verdict and I think the mandatory sentence is appropriate as well."[2]

Michael was sentenced to life imprisonment with a minimum of twenty years to be served before being eligible for parole. A charge of theft for stealing the dynamite added another three years.

When it was time for Barbara's trial, her attorney, Robert Ackerman, requested a change in venue, citing the publicity the case had received. He filed a motion stating the media had covered Michael's trial, making it impossible for her to get a fair trial in Eugene. The request for a change in venue was denied. After a day of jury selection, he once again asked for a change in venue but his request was once again denied. A jury was selected and Barbara's trial got underway with Lane County Circuit Judge Maurice Merten presiding. The state was represented by Lane County District Attorney Brian Barnes.

In his opening remarks to the jury, District Attorney Barnes said, "Barbara Harris hated Rob Harris. Bob Harris was not a raving maniac. Most people who knew him, liked him." He continued on by saying Barbara once told a friend, "I wish he was dead. I've thought about killing him myself." District Attorney Barnes said Barbara told a friend that she tried to poison her husband, but instead of dying, he merely got sick. District Attorney Barnes told the jury Barbara stood to gain $80,000 in life insurance proceeds. He wrapped up his opening arguments by referring to Barbara as "cold blooded and calculated."[3]

Barbara told the court that she loved her husband, was proud of him, and never wanted him dead. Barbara did say that after her husband was killed, she suspected her daughter may have been involved. Robert was convicted years earlier of attempting to rape their daughter and served a stint in prison.

In his closing arguments, District Attorney Barnes stressed to the jury that they were not saying that Barbara was there when the bomb was planted in the car, but she was equally guilty for encouraging the bombing. "If the defendant had not said 'yes' the crime would never have occurred. If the other two guys had not been the kind of guys they were, it probably wouldn't have occurred no matter how much she hated him and wished him dead." In conclusion, District Attorney Barnes said, "The three created a unique combination of neurotic screwballs who together committed a crime none might have done individually."[4]

The trial wrapped up and the jurors began deliberations. After fifteen hours of trying to reach a verdict, the jury foreman told Judge Merten they were unable to reach a verdict on the charge of aggravated murder. The jury did vote 10–2 to convict Barbara of arson. The judge declared a mistrial and ordered that a new trial be held later that year. District Attorney Barnes expressed his disappointment:

> It's no fun to keep trying these cases over and over again. All the people that are here, all the witnesses that are here, all the family that was here; they don't want to have to go through this again. They want to put it to rest. We feel the same way about it, so we always want to get a verdict.[5]

Barbara's attorney requested that Barbara be allowed to post bail and return home. Judge Merten denied the request, writing, "I find the proof is evident and presumption of guilt is strong."

The trial of Terry White began with Lane County Circuit Judge James Hargreaves presiding. Terry was represented by Michael Phillips. Michael Kell had agreed to testify against Terry but when the time came, he refused to testify. Judge Hargraves held him in contempt of court.

A total of seventeen witnesses took the stand. The most damaging evidence the jury heard was Terry's recorded conversation with the Springfield Police Department following his arrest. Terry admitted going to the Rosboro Lumber Company parking lot with Michael, "so Kell could wire up the explosive. I don't have a good reason why I went down there. I just went. I wasn't there as a listening post or anything like that."

On the witness stand, Terry admitted to being at the parking lot with Michael, but claimed he was half asleep and did not know why they were there. He did admit to being present when Barbara and Michael tested a batch of dynamite, but he thought he had talked them out "of the ridiculous idea [of] blowing someone up. What I was concerned about was that the whole plan was insane." Terry testified that he had no idea what Michael had done until later that day when he heard about the car bombing.

The Harris' seventeen-year-old daughter testified against her former boyfriend. She told the jury they had been dating for one month. She said the night before her father was killed, she overheard her mother talking with Terry and Michael. She said Terry asked her mother, "if she wanted him to do away with him, and my mother said 'yes.'" She admitted to the jury Terry told her that he and Michael "went to Rosboro and wired the car up and put some dynamite in there so when my dad got in it in the morning, it would blow up." She also said Terry told her that if she testified, she would end up in foster care and her infant would be removed from her care.

The prosecution and defense rested and the jury began deliberations. It took them five hours to return a verdict of guilty of aggravated murder and arson. Terry showed no outward emotion as the verdict was read.

Terry received a life imprisonment sentence with a minimum sentence of twenty years. He received an additional five years for theft in the first-degree. The theft charge was for accepting parts from Michael off a GMC truck that he stole from Guaranty Chevrolet in Cave Junction.

Terry's conviction was upheld by the Oregon Court of Appeals. At contention was Terry's belief a mistrial should have been declared after the prosecution informed the jury Terry refused to testify against Barbara. He had invoked his rights against self-incrimination and did not feel that should have been presented to the jury during his trial. The appeals court decided in a 6–4 vote that even if the comment had been prejudicial, it was not enough to warrant a new trial.

Barbara's second trial began fourteen months after the car bombing that killed her husband. She took the witness stand and denied having any knowledge of a plot to kill her husband. She further stated she had no idea why others, including her daughter, had said she was in on the plot. She admitted going for a car ride with Michael and Terry the night before the car bombing when they wanted to test a piece of dynamite. She admitted to hearing a loud noise when Michael and Terry were testing the dynamite, but said she "didn't know that's what they were doing or what they had. I didn't know what they were planning to do. I didn't know what was going on."

Barbara told the jury she met Robert when she was thirteen and they married a year later when she found out she was pregnant. She said they have three children. She said she loved her husband and denied ever telling anyone she wished he was dead.

Barbara's second trial resulted in a verdict of guilty of aggravated murder. Barbara placed her head in her hands and wept as the verdict was read. She was sentenced to life in prison with a minimum of twenty years to be served before being eligible for parole. Judge Merten merged her conviction of arson with the aggravated murder conviction. Barbara's attorney filed an appeal but the conviction was upheld.

Terry's case went to the Oregon Supreme Court. They overturned his conviction and ordered that a new trial be held. They found it was incorrect to reveal the fact that Terry had refused to testify at Barbara's trial. They also found that the judge erred in not instructing the jury they could find him guilty of manslaughter instead of murder. They based their finding on that there was evidence that Terry did not intend to commit murder.

Terry's second trial resulted in a guilty verdict. He was once again convicted of aggravated murder and sentenced to life in prison with a minimum of twenty years. His attorney appealed the conviction but the Oregon Court of Appeals upheld the conviction.

21
When the Hitman Tells the Intended Victim

In 2014, Pamela Jean Gygi and Dean Hamill began divorce proceedings. The judge overseeing the divorce ordered that they sell and evenly divide their real property including the custom home they were having built for them on the Oregon coast. Dean was ordered to purchase a $150,000 life insurance policy naming Pamela as the sole beneficiary. Dean left the state of Oregon and began a new life in Utah. He refused to give Pamela his new address.

Pamela met a man from Idaho online and began a long-distance relationship with him. Early on they set a wedding date. Pamela asked her fiancé to find her husband's new address in Utah. The fiancé allegedly hacked into the record system of the Mormon church and secured the address for Pamela. That relationship ended prior to the marriage taking place.

Pamela met another man online and began planning to move to California and marry him. In order to cover these upcoming expenses, she allegedly decided to hire a hitman to murder Dean. She contacted a man she knew from her church. Pamela allegedly gave the hitman $600 and told him where Dean lived. The hitman, however, had no intention of killing Dean.

The hitman was on probation at the time. One of the stipulations of his probation was that he had to remain within the state of Oregon. He decided to violate the terms of his probation and drive to Utah. The hitman had known Dean from when he lived in Oregon. He arrived at Dean's house and informed him that Pamela had put a contract out on his life. On his way back to Oregon, the hitman stopped off in Reno and gambled some of the money Pamela had given him.

Dean went to his local police department—the Saratoga Springs Police Department—and told them what the hitman had said. The detectives with the Saratoga Springs Police Department contacted the hitman who agreed to help them. They also contacted the Springfield Police Department who offered their assistance. Since the crime had crossed state lines, the Saratoga Police Department requested the help of the F.B.I.

The hitman knew if he told Pamela he was not going to kill Dean, she would find someone else to do the job. He continued talking with Pamela and planning the murder. What Pamela did not know was that the hitman was wearing a wire and everything was being recorded.

In one conversation, Pamela allegedly suggested the hitman tamper with Dean's vehicle so that the murder would look like a car accident. That plan was scraped when Pamela became concerned that the accident might only result in an injury, not a death. She was also concerned her son might be a passenger in the car when the accident took place.

In another recorded conversation, the hitman asked Pamela if she still wanted to go ahead with the murder. Pamela allegedly answered in the affirmative. She allegedly told the hitman she would get an untraceable gun for him to use. Pamela allegedly offered the hitman a residence in California, a 2005 Dodge Stratus, and ownership of Dean's online dog and cat breeding business.

On July 10, 2015, Pamela agreed to meet the hitman in the parking lot of a shopping center. She had the 2005 Dodge Stratus on a trailer, which she gave him. She also gave him a gun. At this meeting, she allegedly suggested the hitman make it look like a home invasion robbery. She suggested he steal Dean's rifle, which would make it appear that a home invasion robbery had taken place. The hitman's parting words to Pamela was that Dean would be dead within thirty-six hours. With that, Pamela left the shopping center to go to Costco. The F.B.I. was waiting nearby and video recorded the transaction.

Pamela had barely started on her drive to Costco when special agents from the F.B.I. and detectives with the Springfield Police Department conducted a traffic stop on her vehicle. She was taken in to custody and charged with unlawful firearm possession and interstate commerce to commit facilities in the commission of a murder for hire. Pamela was booked into the Lane County Jail.

Pamela pled innocent to both charges. During her first appearance in federal court, her federal public defender, Bryan Lessley, requested that she be released from jail and placed on house arrest. The judge ruled against the request citing the fact that the allegations against Pamela were significant and she posed a potential threat to Dean.

Pamela pled guilty to a charge of using interstate commerce in a murder for hire plot and possession of an unlawful firearm, meaning that the firearm did not have a serial number. She was sentenced to ten years in federal prison.

22

A Hitman for the Business Partner

Mohdsidek Habibullah, age fifty, and Mohammed Absar, age forty-five, operated a Stop-N-Go Market in southeast Portland. Tensions began running high between the partners. Each partner believed the other owed him money. Also in contention was which partner was putting in more hours operating the store.

Mohdsidek allegedly asked an associate of his to murder his business partner, Mohammed. First the hitman informed Mohammed that his partner wanted to have him murdered. First the associate informed the Portland Police Bureau of the murder for hire plot. Detectives with the Portland Police Bureau asked the potential hitman to wear a wire and record his conversations with Mohdsidek.

In one recorded conversation, Mohdsidek allegedly spoke of wanting the hitman to use a .357-caliber handgun to shoot Mohammed in the head. The Portland Police Bureau arrested Mohdsidek. He was charged with solicitation to commit aggravated murder, criminal conspiracy to commit aggravated murder, and attempted murder.

During Mohdsidek's trial, he told the jury he had been joking when he asked an associate to murder his business partner. The jury believed he was sincere in his attempt to have his business partner murdered and found him guilty of attempted aggravated murder. Mohdsidek was sentenced to fifteen years in prison.

23
The Riley Family

When Gabriel was twelve years old, he was adopted by Lindi and Craig Riley. Lindi worked as a middle school counselor and knew Gabriel when he was a student at Sutherlin Middle School. Gabriel's early childhood was difficult and the Rileys wanted to give him a chance at a better life.

Lindi and Craig lived in Sutherlin for many years. Craig had previously owned an insurance company and had worked as a teacher and basketball coach. Lindi worked at Sutherlin Middle School. In 2003, she was named educator of the year.

At 6:20 on the morning of March 10, 2008, Craig frantically phoned 911 and said he had been attacked; he could smell smoke and the fire alarms were going off in his house. The small town of Sutherlin sent all the resources it had and requested assistance from nearby towns.

The firefighters saw three separate fires as they approached the residence. They saw a trail of blood from the carport to the house and noticed there was blood smeared on the doorknob. As they opened the door, heavy smoke poured out. They began shouting asking if anyone was inside. Craig answered them and they located him on the kitchen floor holding a bloody towel to his neck. They were able to get Craig out of the house and into an ambulance but the fire had grown so quickly they were not able to find Lindi. Once the fire was out, firefighters found her body in a bedroom of the house.

Craig was rushed to Mercy Medical Center in Roseburg. Craig's neck had been slit with a knife. He had also suffered burns on his body. His wounds were so severe that he had to be transferred to Legacy Emanuel Hospital in Portland. He was alert enough to be able to identify the assailant as his adopted son, Gabriel. He told the police, "My son did it. Gabe. My son Gabe." The police immediately began searching for Gabriel. A neighbor told detectives a white pickup sped down the road shortly before the fire broke out. The police quickly learned Gabriel lived in Palm Springs with his wife and two daughters. Gabriel worked in the construction industry.

The police located Craig's pickup truck at Rogue Valley International Airport. They were able to determine Gabriel had taken a flight from Medford to Palm Springs. The Palm Springs Police Department sent detectives to their airport to wait for Gabriel to arrive. As soon as he departed the airplane, he was taken into custody. Gabriel was held on a warrant charging him with aggravated murder, attempted aggravated murder, assault, and first-degree arson. At the time of Lindi's death she was fifty-seven years old. She had worked as a school counselor for twenty-six years. Craig was fifty-seven years old. Gabriel was twenty-nine years old.

Sutherlin Schools Superintendent John Lahley spoke to the media about Lindi, "She was well loved and well known by every single student who went through the middle school." The Riley's pastor, Paul Glazner, spoke about Gabriel's troubled childhood but said, "Lindi had made a real difference in his life." A friend of the family told the police that Gabriel visited his parents on a regular basis. The police learned Gabriel had flown to Oregon for the weekend. One friend told the police Craig, Lindi, and Gabriel had gone out for pizza over the weekend. Another friend mentioned speaking to Lindi on the phone Sunday night, hours before the attack, and hearing Gabriel and Craig laughing in the background.

Gabriel fought extradition but was eventually brought to Oregon. He was booked into the Douglas County Jail and held without bail. The Douglas County grand jury indicted him on all counts.

Before Gabriel's trial began, a fellow inmate of his went to the jail staff with some startling information. The inmate told the authorities Gabriel had offered him money to murder Craig. Gabriel allegedly told the inmate his father was the only eye witness to the crime and he wanted someone to murder him. Based on that information, the Douglas County grand jury indicted Gabriel for solicitation and conspiracy to commit murder.

Gabriel accepted a plea bargain and pled guilty to one count of aggravated murder and one count of attempted aggravated murder. All other charges, including the solicitation and conspiracy to commit murder, were dropped.

Douglas County District Attorney Rick Wesenbberg spoke at the sentencing hearing. He explained that Gabriel stood to inherit his parent's estate. He gave details about the attack:

> He came home to Sutherlin to visit his parents, ostensibly to see them for a weekend. He enjoyed an evening socializing with them, then everyone went to bed. In the early morning hours, Mr. Craig Riley heard his son moving about, acting somewhat odd and talking on his cell phone. He went out to the carport to check on his son, and the defendant at that point came up behind Mr. Riley and attacked him with a knife, slicing his throat.[1]

District Attorney Wesenberg told Douglas Country Circuit Judge Ronald Poole that Gabriel then went back into the house and found his mother asleep in her bed. He used duct tape to bind her hands and then placed a sock in her mouth and applied duct tape over her mouth. He then returned to the carport and discovered his father was still alive. Gabriel "covered him with a tarp, squirted lighter fluid on the tarp, and ignited it." District Attorney Wesenberg described what happened next: "He jumped up on fire, as sort of a ball of fire, ran out in his yard, and dropped and rolled."[2]

Gabriel's defense attorneys, Daniel Koenig and Brad Cascagnette, told Judge Poole their client was taking responsibility for the crimes. They added that by accepting the plea bargain, Gabriel had saved the county a great deal of money by not undergoing a capital murder trial. Judge Poole handed down a sentence of life in prison without the possibility of parole. He added an additional 120 months for the severity of the attack on his father.

At the conclusion of the sentencing hearing, District Attorney Wesenberg told reporters, "A terrible chapter has closed for the Riley family, the people who lived and admired Lindi Riley, and all the people of Douglas County." He added he was happy Gabriel "will die in prison and can never hurt anyone else." He credited the hard work of Detective Jeff Wheaton of the Douglas County Sheriff's Office and Chief Deputy District Attorney Deb Stoll.[3]

When asked by reporters, Craig said he had not spoken to his son since the incident and did not plan to do so in the future. Craig told the reporters, "When I learned about the plea deal, I just sat down in a chair and it was like a weight lifted off my shoulders.

It was a great feeling." He said he purchased a fishing lodge in Canada, adding, "I'm looking forward to getting this behind me and getting out on the water."[4] Craig said he was happy with the resolution of the case.

24
Lance McBride

Sharlene Sheridan returned home after work and discovered her fiancé dead on the kitchen floor of their townhouse. She immediately phoned 911 and officers from the Eugene Police Department arrived at the crime scene. They found Lance McBride, age thirty-five, dead from a gunshot wound. They were able to determine the fatal shot had been fired by someone on the outside shooting through the closed, patio door.

Sharlene was able to provide a few details to the investigators. She told them she and Lance were engaged to be married but she had recently gone through a contentious divorce with her ex-husband, Dennis Richard Sheridan, age forty-one. She explained that she and Dennis had been married for eighteen years and had five children. She said Lance worked as an underground utilities' locator. Sharlene told the police she and Lance were due to be married in a few weeks.

The Eugene Police Department asked the public to come forward if they had any details on the murder. Two weeks into the investigation, the detectives told the media, Lance was "an all-around good guy with no enemies."

Detectives with the Eugene Police Department asked Dennis to come to the police station to answer questions regarding Lance's murder. Dennis arrived at the police station and after a series of questions, he admitted he had discussed different ways to kill Lance with a co-worker, Kevin Bradley Anderson, age twenty-one. He finally admitted he paid Kevin $2,000 to murder Lance. Dennis told the investigators he knew Lance would be home alone because the children he shared with Sharlene were going to be at his house the night of the murder and that Sharlene would be at work.

Once the detectives spoke with Kevin, he admitted Dennis had paid him $2,000 to murder Lance. He told Eugene Police Detectives Ted Williams and Tracey Belshee that he and Dennis had been discussing the possibility of killing Lance for quite a while.

The detectives interviewed a woman who admitted she drove Kevin to Lance and Sharlene's house. She told the investigators she heard a single gunshot at 12:30 a.m., and moments later, Kevin returned to the car, carrying a shotgun.

Both Dennis and Kevin were arrested and charged with aggravated murder. They each pled innocent to the charges. Months later, Dennis agreed to plead guilty to one count of intentional murder, thus avoiding the possibility of the death penalty. He was sentenced to life in prison.

Kevin went from having only had one traffic ticket in his life to facing life in prison for committing murder. He pled guilty to aggravated murder and received a sentence of life in prison with a mandatory thirty years.

25
A Disappearance

Manuel Vasquez' employees became increasingly concerned when he did not show up to work at his farming business, Vasquez Farms. The concern turned to alarm when they located his pickup truck abandoned on the highway outside of Hillsboro. They keys were still in the ignition and the driver's door was wide open. Manual's employees called 911 and asked to speak to the police. The police took a missing person's report. Manuel's office manager told the police he was carrying $3,000 when she last saw him.

What the employees at Vasquez Farms did not know was the police were working behind the scenes and had taken Manuel into police custody upon learning a contract had been put out on his life.

Within weeks of Manuel's disappearance, two men were indicted for conspiring to commit murder. William R. Pewonka, age forty, and Alvin Neal Luttrell, age forty-nine, were indicted by a secret grand jury. At one time Alvin and Manuel had been business partners.

Details emerged showing that William and Alvin had approached another man asking that he murder Manuel. They allegedly paid him $15,000 to kill Manuel. Instead of committing the crime, he went to the authorities and told them everything. William and Alvin were arrested and held in the Washington County Jail. They each faced a $1 million bail.

Manuel was able to return home once the arrests were made. The Washington County Sheriff's Office released a statement saying, "It was necessary for Manuel Vasquez to appear as if he had disappeared to allow the investigation to take its normal course of action." Alvin received a sentence of fifteen years in prison and was ordered to pay a fine of $25,000. William was sentenced to twenty years in prison.

26
A Little Arsenic with Your Coffee

Gerald Robert Price found himself behind bars after a teenage boy went to the police and told them Gerald had hired him to be a hitman. The intended victim of the contract murder was Gerald's wife, Linda. The detectives learned that Gerald, age forty-two, and his teenage son, asked the teenage boy to slip arsenic into the coffee pot at Linda's workplace, Kendall Ford, where she worked as a bookkeeper. The teenage boy also worked at Kendall Ford.

Gerald was arrested and held on $250,000 bail at the Lane County Jail. His son was placed in a shelter for juveniles. Gerald pled innocent to charges of conspiracy to commit murder and solicitation to commit murder.

Gerald's son admitted in juvenile court that he participated in planning his mother's murder. During the juvenile court proceedings, Gerald told the court he had no intention of having his wife murdered, he simply wanted his son to receive the psychiatric help that he needed. He explained that he believed the murder for hire plot would be the best way to get him that help.

During Gerald's trial, the prosecutor laid out what the state believed to be the motive; that being a large life insurance policy. Lane County Assistant District Attorney Frank Papagni told the jury Gerald would benefit from the $154,000 life insurance policy. He blamed Gerald for bringing his son into the murder for hire plot, in an effort to make it appear that he was innocent, and it was all his son's doing. He explained to the jury that the son had a very poor relationship with Linda. "He was the perfect person to select to commit a murder for you because of his love for his father."

One of Gerald's defense attorneys, Shelley P. Smith, told the jury Gerald went along with the murder for hire plot simply to get his son the help he desperately needed. It was Gerald's belief that once his son was arrested, he would have the opportunity to seek counseling services. Shelley explained, "He had no reason to stop it—it was enough for him to know that he had sufficient control that nothing would happen to Linda. He never wanted her dead."

Assistant District Attorney Papagni simply said Gerald's explanation was "Nonsense. The story just doesn't wash." He pointed out that if the arsenic had been added to the coffee pot, other employees of the Ford dealership could have died.

Gerald's son took the witness stand and testified against his father. He told the jury the arsenic was just one of the attempts that had been made on Linda's life. Gerald's son was sentenced to an indefinite period of time at the MacLaren Youth Correctional Facility in Woodburn.

The jury deliberated five hours before returning a verdict in Gerald's trial. The jury found him guilty of conspiracy to commit murder and solicitation to commit murder. During the sentencing phase of his trial, Circuit Judge Donald Kalberer asked Gerald if he had anything to say, to which he replied in the negative. Gerald's wife, the intended murder victim, made one last attempt at convincing the judge Gerald did not intend to harm her, saying, "There's no doubt in my mind." Looking at Gerald, Judge Kalberer quickly replied, "I can't believe she doesn't believe you did what you did. I was satisfied, the evidence was overwhelming you were guilty."

Judge Kalberer told Gerald he took other factors into consideration in deciding his sentence. He explained:

> First, other innocent people could have been injured or killed because of this particular stupid act. And at least as important is the fact that in your foggy mind you attempted to make a murderer out of your son, for whom you profess love. Acts of that nature deserve consideration because it's one thing to do something like that yourself and another to bring in others. You ended up losing the love you wanted to keep—your son—and keeping the love you wanted to throw away—your wife.[1]

Judge Kalberer sentenced Gerald to twenty years in prison with a mandatory eight-year term. Gerald showed no emotion during the sentencing.

27
Buyer Beware

In June 1984, a grand jury indicted Antonio Palacios, age twenty-six, on two counts of solicitation to commit aggravated murder. The indictment stemmed from Antonio's alleged attempt to hire a hitman to murder two detectives with the Woodburn Police Department who had arrested him the previous year on drug charges.

The Drug Enforcement Administration, the Keizer Police Department, and the Polk County Sheriff's Office executed search warrants simultaneously at multiple residences in the Woodburn area. By the end of the day, eight people had been arrested on drug charges. One of those people was Antonio. He was booked into the Marion County Jail on two counts of solicitation to commit aggravated murder and held on a bail of $525,000.

The service of the search warrants concluded a yearlong investigation into Antonio's drug activity and those of his associates. The Oregon State Police and the Woodburn Police Department were the lead agencies in the investigation. By the time they served the search warrants in June, they had spent more than 3,000 hours working the case at a cost in excess of $25,000.

After the simultaneous raids, they were able to locate an additional three people. This brought their total to eleven suspects who were arrested and charged with possession and sales of drugs. The police seized drugs valued at $250,000.

Antonio pled innocent to the charge of solicitation to commit aggravated murder. He was also facing charges of possession and delivery of drugs to which he pled innocent. An undercover police officer purchased heroin from Antonio on two separate occasions.

Woodburn Police Chief Lyle Henderson provided a few details about the solicitation to commit aggravated murder:

> As far as I know, this is the first time in many, many years in the state of Oregon that there has been a contract put on a police officer. Because of the seriousness of the contract, our choice at this time was to go to the grand jury now with our indictments. There's still more charges that will be filed. This isn't the end of the situation.[1]

Oregon State Police Sergeant Lee C. Ericksen told the *Statesman Journal* that Antonio allegedly agreed to pay $12,000 to have a detective with the Woodburn Police Department murdered and a detective with the Polk County Sheriff's Office murdered. Both of the detectives were involved with Antonio's previous arrest for drug possession and sales. Antonio allegedly supplied two guns to the hitman.

What Antonio did not know was that the hitman he hired was an undercover agent with the Drug Enforcement Administration. A trial was held and despite the attempts of the defense, to claim it was a misunderstanding, Antonio was found guilty on two counts of attempted aggravated murder. He was sentenced to forty years in prison. Marion County Circuit Judge Rod Miller filed a recommendation that Antonio not be eligible for parole until he served half of his sentence. Antonio was also found guilty on one count of possession of drugs and two counts of delivery of drugs. The latter was from selling drugs on two occasions to an undercover police officer. He was sentenced to twenty years for the drug charges.

Twenty-four years after Antonio was arrested for hiring a hitman to murder two police detectives, he went before the State Board of Parole and Post-Prison Supervision to be considered for early release. He had been denied an early release previously.

Antonio told the parole board that although he continued using drugs for the first few years in prison, he had not used drugs for the past twenty years. He mentioned he had participated in drug and alcohol abuse programs, bible studies, and a prison program to help youth offenders. Antonio told the board:

> I'm able to talk to youths about my mistakes and the crimes that I committed and all the horrible things I've done. I'm ready to spend the rest of my life in prison because of what I did. That's how I've come to terms with it.[2]

Antonio gave details of his criminal past to the parole board. He admitted the allure of fast cash from drug sales kept him from finishing his business administration degree at Oregon State University. He explained to the parole board, his first drug arrest was in 1981. That case was dismissed due to an error made in the execution of the search warrant. Antonio admitted, "I got lucky." Antonio's first look at the inside of a jail was not enough to prevent him from returning to drug sales. Despite his father's warning that dealing drugs would "bring you to ruin," he continued to deal drugs in the Woodburn area.

Antonio went into detail for the parole board about how he came to hire a hitman. He said two years after his first arrest, he sold drugs to a new customer, unaware the customer was an undercover police detective. The new customer purchased drugs from him on two different occasions. Soon after, he was arrested on possession and delivery of drugs. Antonio said, it was while he was out on bail awaiting his trial that he decided to hire a hitman to murder the two police detectives.

As the parole board listened, Antonio described meeting with the hitman. He admitted giving the hitman guns, drugs and $12,000. The money, he explained, was to be split between the two murders. He paid $7,000 for one of the detectives to be murdered; the other he paid $5,000.

In describing his thought process at the time, he hired the hitman, Antonio said, "I was proud. I was selfish. I was greedy." The reason for hiring the hitman, he explained, was simply to avoid going to prison. He figured if the detectives were no longer able to testify against him, the case would be dismissed. "I didn't want to go to prison. I didn't want to stop selling drugs. I was caught up in that lifestyle."[3]

Antonio said in looking back at the crime, he realized, "I know they were only doing their job. They were trying to get a drug dealer off the streets that was ruining their community." To address his current feelings about the situation, he simply said, "If I have any ill will, it's towards myself because I'm the one that caused all of that to occur."[4]

Marion County Deputy District Attorney Don Abar asked the parole board to take the report from psychologist Robert Stuckey into consideration. After evaluating Antonio, Robert came to the conclusion that Antonio was a danger to society and was severely emotionally disturbed. Deputy District Attorney Abar said, "When we talk about what will prevent Mr. Palacios from release, that psych report is damning."

One of the potential victims testified before the parole board asking that they not be "snowed under" by Antonio's testimony that he had been rehabilitated. The detective went onto say, "I sat here listening to this material that was presented today and I thought 'I've been a cop for 34 years; I'm not buying any of this.'" He told the parole board he had begun carrying a gun all the time in fear that Antonio would be released.

The detective explained to the parole board that Antonio's family was involved in a large-scale illegal drug operation. In addressing his fears about the family's involvement in the murder for hire plot, the detective said, "I think that should really raise some red flags with the parole board … I'm not detrimental to him, I'm detrimental to his entire family."

Antonio admitted to the parole board that some of his relatives did sell drugs decades before, but he insisted they were not part of a large narcotics organization. He emphasized to the parole board, "He says my family was involved. It simply isn't true. As God is my witness, it is not true."

Two of the three members of the parole board voted against granting Antonio an early release from prison, thus ending his bid for freedom. The parole board's report read in part:

> Based on the doctor's report and diagnosis, coupled with all the information that the board is considering, the board concludes that the inmate suffers from a present severe emotional disturbance that constitutes a danger to the health and safety of the community.

The dissenting vote came from one member of the parole board who believed that although Antonio's emotional disturbance was "not presently so severe as to pose a danger to society."[5]

The detective who testified in front of the parole board was relieved to learn Antonio's request for an early release from prison had been denied. He told Alan Gustafson with the *Statesman Journal*:

> I think he deserves to spend every year of his sentence in prison, and as long as I'm alive, I'll keep going back to testify against his early release. I think it's very unfortunate that people throw their lives away. I can feel compassion for him, but he's where he should be. I'm not convinced he's rehabilitated.[6]

Two years later, Antonio went before the parole board once again requesting to be released from prison. Deputy District Attorney Abar stood before the parole board and asked that they deny the early release. The detective who had previously asked that Antonio's request for early release be denied wrote a letter to the parole board. The letter read in part: "In 2008, inmate Palacios was not considered a good risk for release. Nothing has changed. I believe inmate Palacios should pay for his crime … the risk of his committing future acts of violence is too high."[7]

Antonio addressed the parole board. In referencing his intent to harm the two police detectives he said, "I'm sure they went through many sleepless nights." He spoke to his drug use, saying, "I went into that lifestyle and it spiraled out of control."

This time the vote was unanimous—Antonio was granted an early release from prison. Antonio broke into a huge smile and thanked the parole board, saying, "I'll do my very best to not let you down." The parole board reminded Antonio that the good work he had done in prison helping the youth, would not keep him out of trouble on the outside. One member of the parole board told him, "Let me be blunt: On the outside you're a felon, you're an ex-drug dealer."

By the time he walked outside the razor lined fence, he was fifty-one years old. He had been incarcerated for twenty-six years.

28
Margo Compton

"Most people are pretty surprised because nothing ever happens in Laurelwood. Things always happen somewhere else." These were the words spoken by a resident of Laurelwood when a reporter asked her about a local murder.

The police may have felt the same way as they walked into a small house with loaves of freshly baked bread cooling on the counter. They saw two cups of coffee on the table in the living room. Any thoughts they had that nothing ever happens in Laurelwood were immediately dismissed when they came across the bodies of two adults and two children who had been murdered execution-style.

Today, the town of Laurelwood remains a small community and was equally so in 1977 when the murders took place. Most of the residents knew one another or were related to one another. The police first had to determine who the murder victims were. They identified the woman as twenty-five-year-old Margo Compton. The man was identified as nineteen-year-old Gary Seslar. The children were Margo's twin daughters, six-year-old Sylvia and Sandra.

The police were perplexed at how such a brutal murder could occur in the small community of Laurelwood. All four victims had been shot in the head with a small-caliber weapon. The adults were located in the living room. The children were in their bed, still clutching their teddy bears. The murder weapon was nowhere in sight, although the police did notice a number of weapons in the house.

The murders occurred on a hot August day. The front door was wide open, allowing anyone to walk into the house. The house was a small single-story residence down a gravel road. The Washington County Sheriff's Office was summoned to the house when a friend discovered the murders on Sunday evening.

Lieutenant John Vallery of the Washington County Sheriff's Office told the Associated Press, "The homicides appear to be gangland type execution slayings." He added there was no forced entry into the home, and no evidence that anything was stolen. Lieutenant Vallery said there was no sign of a struggle. He told reporters they did not have any suspects nor had they determined how many suspects there were.

Captain Harold Kleve was the head of the detective division for Washington County Sheriff's Office. He took the lead in the investigation. Captain Kleve was quoted as saying:

> It's a very peaceful area nestled down at the foot of the hills out there—a quiet farming area. They don't even steal hubcaps there. It is a small area where everybody knows everybody, but strange as it seems on a Sunday afternoon in broad daylight, no one appears to have seen anyone strange or any strange activity.[1]

The investigators learned Margo had a boyfriend who was out of state at the time of the murders. Margo's boyfriend's son, was the male victim. He was employed by the Coast Guard, but was on leave due to an injury he suffered while riding his motorcycle. He was visiting Margo at the time the killer came to the house.

Bit by bit, the detectives learned more about the victim, Margo. They learned Margo moved to Laurelwood, eight months before the murders took place. She worked at the State Children's Service Division in Hillsboro. Her boyfriend had helped her move to Laurelwood and they were living together. The investigators started piecing together information about where she came from. They learned she had moved from California to Oregon. While in California, she worked as a nude dancer in the Tenderloin area of San Francisco.

Details began to emerge that Margo's desire to leave California was brought on by her life being in danger in California. She had told the authorities her employers were involved with the Hells Angels and they were running a prostitution ring. She said when she tried to quit her job at a nude encounter parlor, they kidnapped her daughters. They ordered her to work as a prostitute or pay them $5,000. She went to the police and told them everything and they were able to return her children to her.

Prior to leaving the golden state, Margo testified before the San Francisco grand jury about her employer's involvement with operating a prostitution ring. After her testimony, the grand jury indicted four males and one female on charges of pimping and pandering. Margo then testified at their trial, which resulted in three of the suspects being convicted.

Margo was scheduled to return to San Francisco and testify against Odis "Buck" Garrett who was facing charges of pimping and pandering. She was murdered days before that could happen. Although Margo did not testify, the jury heard the testimony she gave to the grand jury. Odis was found guilty on a felony charge of pandering. He was sentenced to 1–10 years in prison.

Detectives located tapes that Margo had recorded prior to her death. They also located a diary in which she wrote about her early experiences working at the nude encounter parlor. She wrote:

> At that meeting I was told by Buck that he really didn't think I was cut out to work the hotels as a hooker. That's when he told me about the encounter studio. He told me that it was not prostitution and described it more as counseling.

Once she became involved with the nude encounter parlor, she learned prostitution went for $50 an hour. By that time, she was in too deep to get out. Margo filled seventy-two pages of the diary writing about her experience with drugs and prostitution. In the diary, she did write that she was aware there was a $10,000 contract out for her life for testifying against her former employers.

After Margo was killed, San Francisco Assistant District Attorney Judith Whitmer confirmed that Margo had testified before the San Francisco grand jury about incidents of police corruption. Her testimony was about one San Francisco police officer and one patrolman who was affiliated with the San Francisco Police Department, but was not an employee.

Assistant District Attorney Whitmer said, "All we had was her hearsay statement. We could never establish that money had been paid or that any money was passed." However, she did say that the patrolman who was not an employee of the San Francisco later testified before a federal grand jury. By the end of the trial, eight San Francisco police officers, including a captain, were indicted on federal charges. Also, three owners of night clubs were indicted.

Investigators with the Washington County Sheriff's Office traveled to San Francisco to learn more about their victims. In talking with authorities in San Francisco, they were told a contract had been put out on Margo's life and that the Hells Angels had offered a reward for Margo's murder. They also learned three of the people Margo had testified against, were out on bail.

San Francisco Assistant District Attorney John Dwyer told reporters:

> Revenge could have been a motive. We believe the Angels have killed for much less. But we are sure the case goes deeper than the pimping and pandering charges. It's a strange thing when we find someone like Margo, someone with intimate ties to the underworld, to testify against her own people. I guess we'll never know why she did it.[2]

One law enforcement officer explained the "Angels control the speed and crank [methamphetamine] market on the West Coast." He summed up, "If I had said those things about those guys, I would've been dead by now too."[3]

A former co-worker told *The Oregonian* that the nude encounter parlor where she and Margo worked was "like a supermarket for drugs. And it wasn't the only place the Angels had in the neighborhood for selling speed."

Questions surfaced as to why Margo was not protected from the people she had testified against. San Francisco District Attorney Joseph Freitas told reporter Carol Pogash with *The San Francisco Examiner,* "The police did everything they could legitimately do when she was in our jurisdiction." He added they offered to place her in protective custody, "but she felt it was not necessary because of where she would be" (referring to the rural area in Oregon).

Captain Kleve told reporters from the Associated Press that the Washington County Sheriff's Office was not aware of who she was or that she was living in their jurisdiction until the murders took place. Referring to Margo's safety in Laurelwood, he said, "If she had fears for her safety, she could have called us. With our manpower I don't know if the homicides could have been prevented. We couldn't have given her 24-hour protection." When asked about why she moved to Laurelwood, Captain Kleve said:

> I'd say she was kind of living on the wild side and getting in with the wrong group and was interested in changing and getting out of there. She wanted to break away from that particular group and what they were doing. Laurelwood was a far cry from San Francisco and she had a regular job and seemed to be getting along well.[4]

Margo's ex-husband was awarded custody of the twins two months prior to their deaths. Soon after learning of the murders, he filed a wrongful death claim against the city and county of San Francisco. His contention was the district attorney's office refused to give him Margo's new address in Oregon so he could have her served with the custody papers. He tried to serve Margo when she last visited California to testify at the trial. District Attorney Freitas explained there were laws preventing someone from being served, "When a person comes into our state to testify in a criminal case."

The Oregon Journal received a tip that a $10,000 contract had been put out on Margo's life. The tipster indicated a man from Virginia and a female friend of Margo's from San Francisco drove to Laurelwood. The anonymous source described the female as someone "who was a very close friend of Mrs. Compton and had no idea what was going to be done:"

> This woman friend probably was spaced out on heroin and walked in there with this guy with a big smile on her face and she was as surprised as anybody when the shooting started. I don't think there is much question that the woman friend was killed later too. He probably ditched her body and the car after they left there. She's been missing a week.[5]

The source added that the male usually carried a .22-caliber automatic pistol in his boot. The police recovered seven .22-caliber shell casings at the crime scene.

Another tip led detectives to a couple who were friends with Margo, but the police were unable to locate them. They learned the couple had helped Margo escape from her job at the nude encounter club. The police figured they were either in hiding or had been killed.

One month after the murders, an inspector, William Zerby, with the Solano County Narcotics Bureau told the Associated Press, "I've got a pretty good idea who the murderer is. We're getting closer every day. And when the killers are named, we'll have a strong case. It's not going to happen next week, but it won't take five years either."

Months after making that prediction, William was the victim of a car bombing. He survived the attack which took place hours before he was scheduled to testify at a trial for a member of the Hells Angels who was accused of dealing large quantities of drugs. William told *The Oregonian,* "I wouldn't attempt to separate the attack on me with what happened up there, however." Two men were arrested for the car bombing.

Despite the efforts of law enforcement, Margo's case went cold. Months turned into years and the file folders collected dust. The tips stopped coming in and there was no activity. But then fourteen years after the quadruple murders, two men were indicted by the Washington County grand jury.

One of the men arrested was Odis, who Margo had testified against before the San Francisco grand jury in 1977, days before she was killed. He was arrested and held in the Sacramento Jail in California. The other man who was arrested was Robert McClure. He was located in Stockton and held at the San Joaquin Jail. Both men were charged with four counts of murder. Washington County District Attorney Scott Upham described Robert as a Hells Angels "wannabe."

Washington County District Attorney Upham was interviewed by the Associated Press after the arrests. He said both men had been suspects from the beginning:

> But because of the lifestyles of the people involved and the known violence of the Hells Angels, finding and getting the right people to talk was difficult. Witnesses were terrified to talk because they feared for their lives. People are reticent to disclose those kinds of things.[6]

Washington County District Attorney Upham said that thirteen people testified before the grand jury in this case. Two others, he said, wrote out reports that were presented to the grand jury. He explained that many of the people who testified in front of the grand jury had been placed in protective custody. Others who testified were given new identities in witness-protection plans. He went onto explain that several of the people who testified were in custody on other charges and had to be transferred to Oregon in order to testify and then returned to the prison where they were serving their sentences.

It was another three years before Robert's trial began. By this time, it had been seventeen years since the murders. The pretrial report numbered 9,000 pages, which added to the many delays in preparing the case for a jury trial. Nevertheless, the trial of Robert McClure got underway. The Associated Press covered the trial and newspapers across the country carried the story.

Beginning on the first day of jury selection, and throughout the course of Robert's trial, the Washington County courthouse increased their security in an effort to ward off any potential problems. It was the tightest security any courthouse in Oregon had ever endured. District Attorney Upham told reporters, "A large contingent of Hell's Angels could show up for the trial. Extraordinary security measures are going on." On the first day of pretrial proceedings, one of the highest-ranking members of the Hells Angels was in the courtroom watching the proceedings.

The jury was selected, but due to concerns for their safety, their names were never known, even to those prosecuting the case. Washington County Assistant District Attorney Robert Heard and Assistant State Attorney General Robert Hamilton represented the state of Oregon. Assistant State Attorney General Hamilton told the jury Robert had served time in prison in the 1980s for robbery. It was there in prison that he explained that Robert bragged to his fellow inmates that he was the one who killed Margo, Gary, and the twins. He told the jury that Robert was not a member of the Hells Angels but, instead, was a "wannabe." It was the state's belief that Odis ordered the hit on Margo and her daughters. Gary happened to be at her house at the time but he was not an intended victim.

Assistant State Attorney General Hamilton explained the victims were killed execution style with a .22-caliber handgun. He said Gary was the first to be shot, followed by the girls, all while Margo was forced to watch. She was shot behind the ear three times.

Robert's defense attorney, Lisa Maxfield, told the jury her client was being framed by inmates who wanted to have time shaved off their sentences. Assistant State Attorney General Hamilton countered by saying that none of the witnesses were given a reduction in their sentence, nor had any deals been struck with any of them. He said they simply came forward because two children had been murdered, and that went against even the most hardened criminal.

The prosecution called a parade of prisoners to the witness stand. One after another ambled up to the front of the courtroom in leg irons, handcuffs, and orange jumpsuits and told what they knew. One of the inmates who took the witness stand informed the jury he had participated "directly or indirectly" in twenty-one murders within prisons in California. He spoke of learning that Robert bragged to other inmates about shooting the twin girls. He said the word among the prisoners was that there was going to be a hit placed on Robert because he had killed two children.

All eyes were on a highly ranked leader of the Hells Angels when he took the witness stand. He adamantly denied that the Hells Angels ever ordered a hit on Margo or her children. He denied the Hells Angels were a gang and struck down the prosecution's notion that members of the Hells Angels would retaliate against anyone who testified against them. Instead, he explained, "they get voted out of the club." He added, "I really resent the word 'gang.' We're a motorcycle club."

Reporters with the Associated Press spoke to several members of the Hells Angels who were present in the courthouse. One of the members said, "They're saying this was a Hells Angels hit. We know that wasn't true." Another member told reporters, "Margo Compton meant absolutely nothing to us. She'd already given her testimony. There was nothing to be gained by what happened to her."[7] Another member of the Hells Angels denied they were present in the courtroom in an effort to intimidate the witnesses or the jury.

Regardless of what the members might have believed about the importance of the trial, other law enforcement agencies were watching it with great interest. Sergeant Terry Katz of the Maryland State Police summed it up well by saying, "The Margo Compton case is internationally famous. If you're involved in outlaw bikers in any way, you know the Margo Compton case because of its magnitude and barbarism. It's probably one of the most brutal crimes anywhere." The senior investigator with the New York State Police said he had been following the case because "it's an infamous case in the law enforcement circuit."[8] He added there was a federal court case held in New York wherein the Compton case was admitted into evidence as proof of the Hells Angels retaliation for anyone who testifies against them in a court of law. He said the evidence was allowed even though there had not been any arrests or convictions in the Compton case.

A total of seventy-five witnesses testified during Robert's trial. At the end of the trial, Assistant State Attorney General Hamilton told the jury Robert had made one mistake: He talked to others about the murders. Robert's defense attorney countered that her client was being framed by inmates who wanted to shave time off of their sentences by testifying for the state.

The last of the closing remarks were made and the case was handed over to the jury. After six hours of deliberations the jury returned a verdict of guilty. Robert received four consecutive life sentences. Judge Jon Lund referred to the trial as the "most egregious" murder cases he had ever heard. Speaking to Robert, he said, "You killed four innocent people in a heartless and cold-blooded fashion."

Margo's sister travelled half way across the country to be present for the trial. After the verdict was read, she spoke to reporters about the prosecution team, saying "I believed in these guys. They really knew what they were doing. When you kill children and innocent people, you just can't get away with it." Gary's fiancée also attended the trial. Both women hugged the prosecution team when it was all over.

Assistant State Attorney General Hamilton walked out of the courtroom and said, "I'm relieved because this has been a long, long journey and I'm appreciative to so many, starting with the jury."

Odis was scheduled to go on trial on March 1, 1995, almost a year after Robert's trial ended. At the time, he was charged with the murders that occurred in Oregon, he was serving a life sentence in California on drug charges. His attorneys filed a motion asking the Washington County Circuit Court to dismiss all of the charges against him because his right to a speedy trial had been denied. Their contention was that he was charged with the murders in 1991, but his trial was not scheduled to begin until 1995.

The Washington County Circuit Court did not rule on the motion by the deadline. Odis' attorney took their motion to the Oregon Supreme Court. They in turn gave the

Circuit Court until February 7, 1995, to rule on the motion or show cause as to why they were not going to rule on the motion.

The charges against Odis were not dropped and his trial began in May 1995. The Washington County courthouse was placed on high security. The jurors in this case remained anonymous, just as the ones in Robert's trial. Neither the prosecution, nor the defense were given the names, or any information about the jurors.

Assistant State Attorney General Hamilton began his opening remarks by saying, "The evidence the state will present in this case is the story of this young woman and the story of her death. These killings had been controversial even in the biker community because the killings were of little children. So, from time to time, Mr. Garrett had to explain himself." Referring to the list of witnesses the prosecution planned to call to the witness stand, he said, "We expect you to be incredibly skeptical about the testimony from these violent murderers, robbers, and wife beaters."[9] Assistant State Attorney General Hamilton explained many of the witnesses were willing to come forward because killing small children went against their code of conduct. He emphasized none of the witnesses would be given preferential treatment such as a reduced sentence, dismissal of any charges pending against them, financial support, or immunity in any pending cases.

Odis' court-appointed attorney, Keith L. Walker, was quick to point out that even a trip outside of the prison walls, could make testifying seem worthwhile. Also, knowing that the parole board would see that the inmate had helped the state prosecute a case, could be beneficial when a decision was made about an early release from prison. Keith went onto say he would discredit many of the witnesses saying, "They've become rats and snitches. They are manipulative and they are vindictive."

Many of the witnesses who testified in Robert's trial returned to testify against Odis. Once again, inmates wearing leg irons inched their way to the witness stand. One of the witnesses summed up the reason for his being there by saying, "Snitches should be killed, but their children should not be harmed."

Days before the eighteen-year anniversary of the murders, Odis was convicted of four counts of murder. Odis waived his right to a sentencing hearing. Circuit Court Judge Michael J. McElligott immediately sentenced Odis to four consecutive life sentences. Assistant State Attorney General Hamilton summed the case up by saying:

> This is one of those where you just wonder if it will ever come together, and you just keep plugging away. It's been one of those cases that has had everybody's attention for a long, long time. You send messages in cases like this that if you kill witnesses, let alone witnesses with little girls, we will never quit. We are going to come after you forever.[10]

The International Outlaw Motorcycle Gang Investigators Association honored Assistant State Attorney General Hamilton and Assistant District Attorney Robert Heard for their diligence in prosecuting the case. The association was created to fight motorcycle gangs around the world. The association used the Margo Compton case as an example that it is possible to successfully prosecute cases involving the Hells Angels or similar groups.

Assistant State Attorney General Hamilton gave additional details about prosecuting the case. He mentioned he kept a loaded gun near him at all times, as he never underestimated the danger involved in prosecuting the case. In speaking to the difficulty in making an arrest, he said, "Everybody knows, from day one, this is a Hells Angels hit, but there's no physical evidence." He said the two mistakes they made were killing children and talking about the murder.

It was other inmates willing to talk that finally broke the case, according to Assistant State Attorney General Hamilton. He said members of both the Hells Angels and the Aryan Brotherhood, went to the authorities. The one bit of information that made it believable to law enforcement, he said, was when inmates spoke of the children clutching their teddy bears when they were shot. He said that information had never been released to the public and "it turned out to be a very important corroborating fact that only the killers knew." He went onto say when Odis first learned that Robert was telling his fellow inmates about the murders, he ordered a hit on Robert. The hit never happened for unknown reasons.

"The Hells Angels are the granddaddies of all the outlaw biker gangs" and for that reason it was extremely hard to convince witnesses to testify, according to Assistant State Attorney General Hamilton. He reiterated:

> We made no deals with any of these guys in exchange for their testimony. That was crucial to their credibility in front of the jury. A lot of these witnesses really did risk their lives and will be looking over their shoulders the rest of their lives.[11]

In summing up, Assistant State Attorney General Hamilton sent a warning, "If you attack the system by killing witnesses or judges or police officers or prosecutors, we will never quit. We will always pursue the case."

29

The Rajneeshees

When Bhagwan Shree Rajneesh purchased the Big Muddy Ranch in central Oregon in 1981, no one paid much attention. Yet as more and more people arrived from India, the locals began to take notice. When his investment corporation began buying up huge tracts of land, questions surfaced amongst those who had called this part of Oregon home for generations. When a city began to take shape, complete with an airstrip, the locals could no longer deny that the tiny town of Antelope was being taken over.

Soon hundreds, then thousands of people arrived from India. The locals began hearing that Bhagwan referred to himself as the "Guru of the Rich" and the people who arrived from India were his followers in the commune he set up in Antelope.

Bhagwan operated a commune in Poona, India where he had thousands of followers. In America, he had a commune in Berkeley, California and another in Los Angeles. He referred to his followers as "sannyasins." His followers dressed in orange or red clothing and wore necklaces made of wooden beads known as a "mala." In the center of the necklace, there was a photograph of Bhagwan. They referred to Bhagwan as "Master." The followers did not receive wages, and in fact many turned over their savings to

Bhagwan in exchange for "mutual support and acceptance." It was not unusual for the followers to turn over their worldly goods to Bhagwan's foundation.

He chose the remote region in Oregon for another commune. He paid $6 million in 1981 for the 68,000-acre Big Muddy Ranch. The property stretched between Wasco and Jefferson counties. Bhagwan's followers began clearing 2,000 acres of land that they planted in sunflowers, corn, and zucchini. The main source of income for the commune was the sale of tapes and video recording of Bhagwan that were sold around the world. In the recorded tapes and videos, he spoke of his beliefs and the importance of meditation and proper breathing techniques.

Bhagwan did not interact with the locals but they saw him being driven by his followers in one of his two Rolls Royce automobiles. Bhagwan's manager, Sheela Silverman, explained the need for two Rolls Royce cars, was in case one was at the mechanics undergoing repairs. "The Bhagwan is so sensitive, I would not expect him to ride in anything less." Within months after arriving in Oregon, Bhagwan celebrated his fiftieth birthday. His followers ordered a cake from a bakery in Bend. The cake was decorated with the words: "Happy Anniversary to our beloved Master." The cost of the gigantic cake was $1,020.

Within months of the purchase of the Big Muddy Ranch, Bhagwan filed a petition with Wasco County to incorporate a new city near the town of Antelope. Bhagwan proposed naming the new city, Rajneeshpuram. Every resident of Antelope attended the Wasco County commissioner's meeting and voiced their opposition. The officials representing the commune voiced their need for a city so they could build a health clinic, a library, a school, and stores to serve the needs of their community. The county commissioners left the decision to the voters. The locals knew they were greatly outnumbered and the members of the commune would succeed in voting to incorporate a city.

Seemingly overnight, a city began to appear once the voters approved the new city of Rajneeshpuram. This was despite the many efforts of the locals to prohibit the building of a city. The locals filed numerous legal challenges desperately trying to block the growth but were not successful in their endeavors. Soon, Bhagwan's followers held all but one elected city office. They claimed that anyone could live in Rajneeshpuram, therefore they were not breaking any laws.

Funds to build the city came from around the globe, all sent by Bhagwan's followers. His worldwide followers were thought to number past 250,000. The cost to build Rajneeshpuram was estimated at $50 million. Bhagwan also had other investments in Oregon.

Each summer, thousands of followers would descend on central Oregon to attend the Rajneeshpuram World Celebration. The cost to attend ranged from $500 for eight days, all the way to $3,000 to stay for three months. The fees covered the cost of food, a tent, and transportation from Portland. Attendees had to pay extra for workshops said to improve their "meditation and inner growth." For additional fees, they could sit in a large building with the self-proclaimed guru. However, since he had gone silent soon after arriving in Oregon, the attendees would not gain any insight from his words. He told his followers his need for silence was the last portion of his work and the day would come that they, too, could sit in silence with him. A spokesperson for the festival said they expected to net a $3 million profit from the event.

In 1983, the Rajneesh Investment Corporation purchased a four-story hotel in Portland. They also bought a bakery and a nightclub and restaurant. They had only owned the 127-room hotel for a few months when bombs exploded at the renamed Hotel Rajneesh in Portland. The police learned someone had phoned the hotel and spoke to one of Bhagwan's followers days before the bombing. The anonymous caller said he planned to hire someone to murder Bhagwan.

In 1984, Bhagwan and his followers wanted to take control of the Wasco County Board of Commissioners. In order to do so, they decided to bolster the number of registered voters. Knowing that each voter was required to be a resident of the county for twenty days prior to casting a vote, they worked on bringing additional people to the commune. They planned to write in the names of two followers on the ballot. Soon busload after busload of homeless people arrived at the commune. By the deadline, it was estimated that 3,500 homeless people had completed the required voter registrations. A follower who went by the name of "Sunshine" was asked by reporters if the new arrivals would be allowed to stay indefinitely at the commune. Sunshine replied they were "welcome to stay the rest of their lives, as long as they abide by the community's rules against violence, crime, and possession of drugs." In reality, many were bused to Portland and dropped off without any food or money. The local Salvation Army stepped in to assist and asked for the public's help.

As it turned out, Wasco County issued a blanket rejection of all new voter registrations. Bhagwan's attorney filed a lawsuit in federal court claiming their rights were being violated. In a last-minute effort to keep the residents of The Dalles from voting, Bhagwan's followers allegedly spread salmonella across salad bars at ten restaurants in The Dalles. More than seven hundred people became ill. The residents suspected the commune was involved. They made every effort to cast their votes, regardless of how sick they were. The 9th U.S. Circuit Court of Appeals rejected their lawsuit. In the end, they did not win the election and withdrew their lawsuit in the interest of "spirit of peace."

One of the locals went on the Merv Griffin television show and talked about Rajneeshpuram. Soon after, Anand went on a Portland radio show and criticized the woman for talking about the commune on national television. The commune had their own newspaper, the *Rajneesh Times*. They used that medium to blast the woman. They also filed a defamation lawsuit against the woman. She in turn filed a counter suit. Multnomah County Circuit Court Judge Clifford Olsen ruled in the woman's favor. In his ruling, he called Anand's statements malicious and added they "could hurt the woman."

Legal troubles soon surfaced. The U.S. Immigration and Naturalization Service began legal proceedings to deport Bhagwan claiming his tourist visa had expired. His followers, many of whom were attorneys, filed documents stating Bhagwan should be granted permanent residence as a skilled worker.

The U.S. Immigration and Naturalization Service was also looking into the status of hundreds of marriages. Their contention was the number of U.S. citizens who supposedly were marrying Bhagwan's followers, thus seeking permanent residency in the United States. The followers claimed they were being discriminated against. Throughout the legal proceedings, Bhagwan refused to testify, citing his vow of silence.

In 1984, Bhagwan's first assistant, Anand, was arrested by federal agents. She was convicted of the bioterror attack regarding the salad bars, as well as a charge of attempted murder. She served twenty-nine months in a federal prison in California. Once she was released, she fled to Switzerland.

After Anand was arrested, investigators uncovered what they believed was the largest wiretapping case in the history of Oregon. They confiscated thousands of cassette recordings from the commune. The Wasco County grand jury indicted twenty-one of Bhagwan's followers for the wiretapping.

Investigators next learned of a conspiracy to commit murder on Bhagwan's personal doctor. His followers also allegedly attempted to commit murder on an Oregon politician. Investigators were still reeling from this information when they uncovered a plot by Bhagwan's followers to allegedly fly a plane filled with bombs into the Wasco County courthouse.

Federal agents believed Bhagwan was attempting to flee the United States by flying to Bermuda to escape the pending charges against him. When two private Lear jets arrived in Charlotte, North Carolina, Bhagwan and six of his followers were taken into custody. Bhagwan pled innocent to all charges. He put up 10 percent of his $500,000 bail and was released from custody. Fearing Bhagwan had the means to fly undetected out of the United States, federal prosecutors ordered all airplanes capable of long-distance flights to be removed from the Rajneeshpuram airstrip.

Facing numerous charges, Bhagwan accepted a plea bargain. In doing so, he pled guilty to one count of conspiracy to arrange a sham marriage and one count of lying to the U.S. Immigration and Naturalization Service. The other thirty-two charges against him were dropped. Part of his plea agreement was he could not return to the United States for five years. He was fined $400,000 to cover some of the costs incurred by the state. Through one of his attorneys, Rajneesh told the media that he still "asserts his innocence."

His followers lined the road, singing and cheering one last time as Bhagwan's chauffer drove him out of town on the way to the airport. He stepped out of the silver Rolls Royce and bowed to the followers who were waiting at the airport. By this time, he had acquired more than ninety Rolls-Royce automobiles. Bhagwan flashed a victory sign and then got into a private Cessna airplane that took off in the sky, leaving behind his confused and angry followers. One of his spokespersons said, "I'm at the same time sad and relieved. I'm sad for this country and what they have done to him. I'm relieved that he can get out of here."

U.S. Attorney for the District of Oregon Charles Turner was quoted as saying, "The legacy of crime that this man left behind is unparalleled in American jurisprudence." Oregon Governor Vic Atiyeh referred to Bhagwan as "a charlatan and a very evil person. Evil in the sense of the kind of people he gathered around him and what he allowed them to do, and his own personal arrogance. He was above everything." Oregon Secretary of State Norma Paulus summed up the situation by saying, "At the time we were going through it, we didn't realize how extraordinary it was. I can't think of any comparable incidents in American history."[1]

Investigators learned Bhagwan's followers had conspired to murder U.S. Attorney Turner. The plan was to kill him in a parking garage near the courthouse in Portland. They believed by killing him, the investigation into the sham marriages would cease. They learned a group of followers had purchased weapons out of state and transported them via Greyhound bus to avoid metal detectors in airports. The group purchased three Ruger .357-caliber Magnum revolvers and a Colt .38-caliber revolver.

Later that year, Carol Matthews, age forty, was arrested in Germany. Catherine Jane Stubbs, age forty-five, and Richard Kevin Langford, age forty, were arrested in West Germany. The police located Ann Phyllis McCarthy, age forty-three, in South Africa. Susan Lissanevitch, age forty-three, and Sally-Anne Ann Croft, age forty, were arrested in England. Extradition proceedings began to bring the six individuals back to America to stand trial for conspiracy to commit murder, wiretapping, and interstate transportation of firearms.

Ma Anand Sheela, age forty-five, was indicted as well. The investigators learned she had married Urs Birnstiel, a native of Switzerland. Urs fled to his native Switzerland after being indicted on a federal wiretapping charge in Portland involving Bhagwan. By marrying Urs, Ma became a citizen of Switzerland, thus eliminating any chance she would be extradited to the United States. In the end, she was tried in Switzerland and was found guilty of criminal acts preparatory to the commission of murder. She received a sentence of time served.

Carol and Richard were extradited to the United States to stand trial for five counts of wiretapping. They both entered pleas of innocent. Richard pled guilty and was sentenced to five years in prison. He agreed to testify against others involved in the conspiracy to commit murder. Carol entered an Alford plea and was sentenced to five years in prison. Ann pled guilty to conspiracy to commit murder and was sentenced to one year in jail. U.S. Attorney Turner referred to the sentence as "laughable."

A judicial court in Germany refused to extradite Catherine. She claimed the conspiracy to commit murder and her alleged role in the conspiracy were no longer valid because she had left the United States. Chief Criminal Assistant U.S. Attorney Baron Sheldahl told the media the arrest warrant would remain in effect and if she ever left Germany, they would attempt to have her arrested.

Years later, Catherine agreed to return to the United States. In exchange for returning to the United States, she was allowed to fly to Australia to visit her terminally ill adult son. Once back in the United States, she pled guilty to conspiracy to commit murder and violation of federal firearms laws. A federal prosecutor referred to Catherine as the "MVP" of the conspiracy to commit murder. Catherine admitted to conspiring to murder U.S. Attorney Turner and apologized for her involvement in the plot. She was sentenced to five years' probation and was allowed to return to Germany. U.S. Attorney Turner was quoted as saying, "This was a lying-in-wait conspiracy to murder me, a presidential appointee, and for a long time I slept with a loaded gun beside my bed." U.S. District Judge Malcolm Marsh told the prosecutors he believed Catherine had seen the "errors of her ways."

In 1994, Sally-Anne Croft and Susan Hagan landed in America after fighting extradition for four years. They fought extradition based on their claim they would not be able to get a fair trial in Oregon due to the publicity. The *Daily Telegraph* in London reported:

> As to why the Oregon authorities should be interested in prosecuting members of a cult which left the state eight years ago, the answer seems to be that it is the quickest route to the hearts and votes of the red-neck residents of America's Bible Belt.[2]

The women took their fight all the way to the appellate court in England. The judges there signed the extradition papers. The two women were flown to the United States to face charges of conspiracy to commit murder on a federal officer.

When their trial finally got underway, their defense attorneys told the jury they would hear from witnesses who were former followers of Bhagwan. They warned the jury the witnesses had changed their stories over the years and were only testifying to benefit their legal cases. The lead prosecutor for the government was T. J. Reardon. He opened by telling the jury, "One overt act is needed to prove the crime of conspiracy. We will have for your consideration a number of overt acts."

The first witness was David Knapp, the self-proclaimed former mayor of Rajneeshpuram. He told the jury both women were present when the first mention of killing U.S. Attorney Turner was brought up. The defense attorneys presented a transcript of David's interview with the F.B.I. wherein he failed to mention Susan was present. "I recall Sally-Anne saying that she could provide money for that if it was necessary." David said as the idea of killing U.S. Attorney Turner gained momentum, a group of followers began surveillance. They watched his house and office and tracked his comings and goings. He told of a time the group pretended their car broke down near U.S. Attorney Turner's house as a ploy to be able to conduct surveillance on his house. David admitted he used a tiny camera and took a photograph of U.S. Attorney Turner while he was at a conference in Sunriver. David also said a group went to Texas and New Mexico and purchased weapons. He said the group of followers met every day and continued to plan the murder. He told the jury, "I recall Su making a statement encouraging the people there by saying, 'Look, we have to do something here. We have to support Sheela. We have to make sure the commune does not go down the drain.'"

The weapons allegedly purchased to carry out the murder were introduced into evidence. They had been located from a lake that was drained after authorities learned of their location at the bottom of a lake in Rajneeshpuram. It was the government's belief Sally-Anne provided the funds from the commune's resources to purchase the weapons. Photographs allegedly taken by the group that depicted U.S. Attorney Turner's house were introduced into evidence.

After a long trial, the jury began deliberations. After three days they returned a verdict of guilty of conspiracy to commit murder. When reporters reached U.S. Attorney Turner, he commented on the verdicts saying, "vindicate the rule of law and they say public officials should be able to conduct the public business without fear and intimidation." He said he felt no ill will towards any of the defendants in the case.

Sally-Anne and Susan were sentenced to five years in prison for their part in the conspiracy to commit murder plot. Their attorneys filed an appeal but the 9th U.S. Circuit Court of Appeals upheld their conviction. The women were released from prison after serving three years. In January 1990, Bhagwan died in Poona, India, of apparent heart failure.

30

Payment: Cash and Car Parts

On November 4, 1988, a hunter came across a van on a remote gravel road outside of Lake Creek. Deputies from the Jackson County Sheriff's Office arrived on scene and discovered the body of Donna Mae Richards inside the van. She had been beaten and stabbed to death.

The night before, Donna's husband, Charles, had reported her missing. He told the deputies from the Jackson County Sheriff's Office that she had left the house three hours earlier to help a relative jumpstart his truck in Phoenix.

Details soon emerged that the marriage was fractured. Within days the detectives learned that Charles was so concerned that Donna was going to leave him and take everything, that he hired two men to kill his wife. In exchange for killing his wife, Charles offered them money and car parts. Charles figured that he would inherit his wife's estate if she was dead, as opposed to being penniless if Donna divorced him. Charles was fifty-five years old and Donna was fifty-four years old at the time of the murder.

Just four days after the discovery of the body, Charles and one of the hitmen were arrested and held on a charge of aggravated murder. Days later, the police located the second hitman in Colorado and took him into custody. He was charged with aggravated murder and conspiracy to commit murder. His wife was charged with hindering prosecution after lying to the police about her husband's whereabouts.

One of the hitmen told investigators that Charles offered to pay the two of them in cash and car parts if they would murder his wife. The hitman admitted the two of them lured Donna to Phoenix on the pretense of a broken-down car that would not start. The hitman told the investigators they killed Donna on a remote road near Lake Creek. He described in detail how he hit Donna repeatedly with a hammer. He said when Donna began to regain consciousness, he hit her with a saucepan. He then stabbed her before hitting her again with the hammer. He said they left her in the van which they parked down a gravel road outside of Lake Creek.

Jackson County District Attorney Bill Juba decided to not pursue the death penalty. Instead, because it was a murder for hire, he charged them with aggravated murder and non-aggravated murder. He and defense attorney Bert Putney agreed to forego a jury trial, instead asking a judge to decide the case.

Judge Loren Sawyer convicted one of the hitmen of aggravated murder and sentenced him to life in prison with a minimum of thirty years to be served before he would be eligible for release. The other hitman was sentenced to life in prison, with a minimum of thirteen years. Charles pled guilty to non-aggravated murder. He received life in prison with a minimum of twenty-five years.

31
The Need to Hire a Hitman to Murder a Hitman

One day while talking to friend in the parking lot of a local gym, Bourne Paraday Huddleston, age forty-three, casually asked his friend if he would be willing to murder his wife. Bourne offered to pay him $20,000 to commit the murder, explaining that he would receive $60,000 from life insurance proceeds once his wife Kristy was dead. Bourne was friends with the young man from the gym and also from school. They were studying to be paramedics at the local community college. The friend told Bourne he would think about it.

The following week, the friend informed Bourne that he was not interested in committing the murder, but his cousin might be willing to do so. The two of them met the cousin at a local McDonald's restaurant. After listening to the details of how Bourne wanted the murder done, the cousin declined the offer of $10,000 to murder Bourne's wife. During the meeting, Bourne spoke of having killed in the past. Bourne had recently retired from the U.S. Marine Corps. He served twenty-nine years and was deployed to the Middle East four times.

Just before 2 a.m. on the morning of March 23, 2012, Bourne's ten-year-old son was awoken by a loud scream. He got out of bed and opened his bedroom door. As he walked into the hallway, his father suddenly rushed past him, carrying an assault rifle. Bourne told the child to go back to bed, which he did, but once he heard his dad's truck start up and leave the driveway, he went into his parent's bedroom.

He found his mother covered with a sheet and a pillow over her head. He turned on the light and saw there was blood everywhere. He found her cellphone nearby and phoned 911. He described to the 911 operator that his mother had a cut on her neck and that his father had left the house to go get the police but he did not think he would be coming back for a while.

The 911 operator asked the child to check for a pulse and to place his mother on her back. The 911 operator walked the ten-year-old boy through steps for CPR. He did a remarkable job administering CPR to his mother while waiting for help to arrive. The child continued performing CPR but at one point he simply said it was too late, she was gone.

Deputies Steven Scow and Ben Fazio from the Jackson County Sheriff's Office were the first to arrive on scene. They immediately began CPR on Kristy. Within minutes, personnel from Mercy Flights, firefighters from Fire District 5, and troopers with the Oregon State Police arrived on scene. Additional life-saving measures were taken, but Kristy succumbed to her injuries. Deputy Medical Examiner Randy Arnold arrived on scene and determined that Kristy had been shot once below the left ear.

The child told the deputies that his father had left the house and was driving a large red pickup truck. He gave the deputies his father's cell phone number. Deputies from the Jackson County Sheriff's Office placed an emergency ping on Bourne's cell phone. Within minutes, they were notified the cell phone was pinging in the nearby town of Eagle Point (approximately 20 miles away).

A large contingent of law enforcement went to the address where the cell phone was pinging. They located Bourne outside in a cul de sac. He was immediately taken into custody. Bourne calmly asked what was going on. Deputy Jesus Murillo with the Jackson County Sheriff's Office told Bourne something had happened at his house. Bourne asked if his son and wife were okay. Deputy Murillo informed Bourne that his son was fine and more details would be forthcoming. As he was being led to the sheriff's vehicle, Officer LaFord with the Eagle Point Police Department spotted a grip portion of a pistol hidden in a nearby bush, a few feet from Bourne's truck. There was a black glove attached to the partial gun.

Bourne was taken to the Jackson County Sheriff's Office and interviewed by Detectives Charlie Retzer and Eric Fox. Bourne wasted no time explaining to the detectives that he was engaged to be married to a young lady, even though he was still legally married to Kristy. He explained he was at his fiancé's house when he was arrested. Bourne told the detectives he was at home with Kristy when she shot herself in an attempt to commit suicide. He said had just closed the bedroom door when she picked up a gun and he heard a gunshot. Bourne said he panicked and did not know what to do, but he did get a wet washcloth and wipe off her hands and his hands. His explanation for this was so there would be no gunpowder residue as he did not want her family to know she had taken her own life. He said he thought about taking her body from the house so it would look like she had been murdered, but instead he fled the house. He admitted seeing his son in the hallway and telling him to go back to bed. Bourne admitted to tossing part of the gun out the window as he drove to his fiancé's house and then hiding the rest of it in the bushes. Bourne emphasized, "I didn't do it … I didn't shoot her! I tried to think what am I going to do. How am I going to make it look like I didn't do this." When the interview was finished, Bourne was booked into the Jackson County Jail.

Deputy Ian Lance with the Jackson County Sheriff's Office took the child to the Children's Advocacy Center and interviewed him regarding what he had seen and heard. Kristy's parents arrived and took him to their house. Bourne pled not guilty to murder, attempted aggravated murder, soliciting murder, soliciting aggravated murder, and possession of a silencer. He was denied bail and returned to the Jackson County Jail.

Kristy's family and friends mourned the loss of this beautiful young mother. Kristy worked as a nurse case manager for the Department of Veteran's Affairs Southern Oregon Rehabilitation Center. She helped veterans returning from active duty to acclimate after being deployed. Her supervisor summed up Kristy's abilities best by saying, "Wow, there's Kristy and there's everyone else." Kristy earned her bachelor degree in nursing followed by her master's degree in nursing. She was one step away from earning her Ph.D. in nursing. Kristy taught nursing classes at the University of Phoenix. Ten years before her death, she gave birth to Bourne's son. This was her only child. Her son was the light of her life. She took him on special dates every week, such as going to a movie or going to a restaurant.

It did not take long for the investigators to uncover the two murder for hire plots. The first potential hitman came forward and told Detective Steve Holthus with the Jackson County Sheriff's Office everything he knew about the case. He told Detective Holthus that Bourne had offered him $5,000 to be his alibi after he turned down the offer to commit the murder. The hitman said he received a text message from Bourne twenty minutes before Bourne was arrested saying he had earned the $5,000. This was allegedly an apparent covert way of telling him he needed the alibi.

The second potential hitman told Detective Holthus Bourne came off as being very arrogant at their meeting. He said he was offered $10,000 to murder Kristy and Bourne had told him he would be paid once Bourne received the life insurance proceeds. He told the detective that Bourne described a scenario wherein the murderer could shoot his wife from a vacant field across from his house when she pulled into the driveway and got out of her car. The hitman said when he declined the offer, Bourne indicated he would find someone else to murder his wife.

Bourne had not been behind bars long when jail authorities uncovered yet another murder for hire plot. This time, Bourne allegedly asked a cellmate if he would be willing to kill one of the potential hitmen. Bourne allegedly said he needed the hitman out of the way so he would not be able to testify against him. In addition, to this request, he also wanted "something to happen" to Deputy District Attorney Dave Hoppe. Bourne allegedly offered a few suggestions including using the poison, Succinylcholine. Deputies knew Bourne was familiar with this particular drug because they found a vial of it in Bourne's house the night Kristy was murdered. Bourne allegedly offered his cellmate $3,000 if he would take out both people.

In addition to this, Bourne allegedly asked his cellmate to find him someone who would testify that he was at the Huddleston's front door when he observed Bourne standing in the kitchen. The alibi witness was to say he was looking through the glass front door when he heard a gunshot. He would then need to say he observed Bourne jump when he heard the gunshot and then he rushed from the room.

As the authorities were unraveling Bourne's latest plot, they discovered he was calling his sister in Florida. Even though inmates can make phone calls, there are large signs in the jail warning the inmates that all calls are recorded and monitored. Bourne brought his sister into his latest murder for hire plot. She allegedly agreed to help Bourne. He then brought another sister into to this ever increasingly bizarre plot.

Bourne's cellmate worked with law enforcement, and together, they created a scenario wherein Bourne was informed the hitman had been killed. The cellmate called Bourne's sister in Florida and used the term "Independence Day," meaning the hitman was dead. Bourne's sister allegedly wired $1,000 to the cellmate for the "purchase of a motorcycle." The cellmate, accompanied by Detective Holthus and Detective Eric Fox, picked up the wire transfer at a local Fred Meyer store.

The investigators learned that one of Bourne's sisters sent a blank check to Bourne's fiancé. The fiancé allegedly wrote out the check for $3,000 and gave $2,000 cash to the cellmate for a "motorcycle."

Special Agent Jeff Gray with the F.B.I. flew to Florida to interview one of Bourne's sisters. She admitted to knowing details about the case. Special Agent Gray informed her the would-be hitman was missing. She denied having any knowledge of his whereabouts. She admitted to being involved with the money for "the motorcycle." When Special Agent Gray informed her that the cellmate was cooperating with the police and he wanted to play the recorded phone calls, she immediately said she wanted to speak to an attorney. The interview was terminated. The grand jury indicted Bourne and his sister on charges of conspiracy to commit murder and attempted murder.

Bourne's trial got underway two years after Kristy was murdered. Deputy District Attorney Laura Cromwell and Deputy District Attorney David Hoppe represented the state of Oregon. Bourne was represented by defense attorney Robert Abel. Jackson County Circuit Judge Lorenzo Mejia presided over the case.

"Like a coward, I ran out of the room. I ran." Bourne spoke those words to the jury and a packed courtroom when he took the witness stand in his own defense. He explained that Kristy shot herself in an apparent suicide attempt. He told the jury he washed the gunpowder off Kristy's hands to spare her family from learning she had taken her own life. He admitted to lying to the detectives when he was first arrested, adding that he lied because he was scared.

The prosecutors honed in on why Bourne failed to render aid to his wife or to call 911 in as much as he had just passed his certification hours before to be an emergency medical technician. He did not have an explanation for why he left the house instead of rendering aid. Before Bourne left the witness stand, he said, "I have prayed every day for my son's forgiveness for what I did to him."

State Medical Examiner Dr. James Olson testified that Kristy could not have shot herself because there were no searing, soot, or powder articles on her skin surrounding the bullet wound. He also spoke of the trajectory of the bullet and how the gun would have been fired. Bourne had insisted that Kristy shot with her left hand, even though she was right-handed. Dr. Olson explained to the jury the gun would have been fired from the right.

It did not take long for the jury to return guilty verdicts on all ten charges. Bourne was sentenced to life in prison, with a minimum twenty-five years. Judge Mejia recommended that if Bourne were to be released that he remain on post-prison supervision for the rest of his life. Looking at Bourne, Judge Mejia said:

> I have never made that recommendation ... I have never seen anyone like you. You are a person who is amoral, anti-social, you have a lack of ability to love, to be empathetic to anybody, and your primary and only concern is yourself and your needs ... I feel sorry for your mother, I feel sorry for your son, I have no sympathy for you, sir ... It is my hope and desire that you spend the rest of your life in prison.[1]

Kristy's parents were awarded custody of the ten-year-old child. Kristy's mother addressed the court at Bourne's sentencing:

> My main concern has been my grandson—what he went through for months and months. Nightmares, waking up terrified that his father was going to come back and kill him too. I don't know why you couldn't be a man and just walk away from my daughter instead of taking her life and putting my grandson through that.[2]

Bourne's sister pled guilty to one count of solicitation to commit murder. A plea bargain was reached wherein eight other charges against her were dropped. She received a sentence of five years' probation. She was allowed to return to her home state of Florida with the understanding if she violated the terms of her probation, she would have to serve three years in a prison in Oregon.

Part of Bourne's sister's plea bargain was that for her to avoid being sent to prison, Bourne agreed to plead no contest to a third charge of attempted aggravated murder. This added thirty years to Bourne's sentence, thus ensuring that he would spend the rest of his life in prison. Also, as part of the plea bargain, Bourne signed notarized documents stating he would never attempt to lay claim to Kristy's estate. Instead, the money would go to their son.

Endnotes

Chapter 1

1 *Albany Democrat-Herald*, February 2, 1973, p. 2.
2 Hawkins, J., *The Capital Journal*, March 2, 1973, p. 1.
3 Shephard, R., *The World*, March 2, 1973, p. 1.
4 *Ibid.*
5 *Statesman Journal*, February 10, 1987, p. 1.
6 *The Napa Valley Register*, August 25, 1987, p. 2.
7 Mulady, K., *The Sacramento Bee*, March 2, 1988, p. 12.
8 *The Sacramento Bee*, March 23, 1988, p. 10.
9 *Santa Cruz Sentinel*, March 28, 1988, p. 14.
10 *The Sacramento Bee*, September 28, 1989, p. 18.
11 *Albany Democrat-Herald*, October 3, 1989, p. 5.
12 Jackson, S. P., *Statesman Journal*, March 23, 1990, p. 1.

Chapter 2

1 *Statesman Journal*, September 16, 1989, p. 2.
2 *Ibid.*, p. 5.
3 *Statesman Journal*, September 21, 1989, p. 3.

Chapter 3

1 *Statesman Journal*, February 24, 1982, p. 1.
2 Evenson, J., *Statesman Journal*, March 27, 1982, p. 4.
3 Evenson, J., *Statesman Journal*, July 24, 1982, p. 1.
4 Evenson, J., *Statesman Journal*, July 27, 1982, p. 1.
5 *Ibid.*
6 *Ibid.*, p. 10.
7 *Ibid.*
8 *Ibid.*, p. 4.
9 *Ibid.*, p. 3.
10 Evenson, J., *Statesman Journal*, July 28, 1982, p. 1.
11 *Ibid.*
12 Evenson, J., *Statesman Journal*, July 29, 1982, p. 1.
13 *Ibid.*
14 *Ibid.*
15 *Ibid.*
16 Evenson, J., *Statesman Journal*, August 5, 1982, p. 5.
17 *Ibid.*
18 Evenson, J., *Statesman Journal*, August 6, 1982, p. 1.
19 *Ibid.*
20 *Ibid.*
21 *Ibid.*

22 *Statesman Journal*, November 11, 1982, p. 10.
23 *Statesman Journal*, February 23, 1982, p. 32.
24 *Statesman Journal*, July 15, 1991, p. 20.

Chapter 4
1 *Statesman Journal*, April 10, 1980, p. 28.
2 Lipka, M., *Statesman Journal*, December 5, 1982, p. 2.
3 *Ibid.*
4 *Ibid.*
5 *Albany Democrat-Herald*, December 30, 1982, p. 15.
6 *Albany Democrat-Herald*, August 5, 1985, p. 1.

Chapter 5
1 Postrel, D., *Statesman Journal*, July 17, 1988, p. 3.
2 *Ibid.*
3 *Ibid.*, p. 4.

Chapter 6
1 *Corvallis Gazette-Times*, October 14, 1984, p. 5.
2 *Corvallis Gazette-Times*, January 22, 1985, p. 1.
3 *Ibid.*
4 *Corvallis Gazette-Times*, January 23, 1985, p. 11.
5 *Ibid.*
6 *Corvallis Gazette-Times*, January 31, 1985, p. 12.
7 *Albany Democrat-Herald*, February 1, 1985, p. 10.
8 *Statesman Journal*, December 25, 1986, p. 2.

Chapter 7
1 MacDonald, J., *The Province*, March 14, 1982, p. 1.
2 *Spokane Chronicle*, April 19, 1984, p. 1.
3 *Albany Democrat-Herald*, May 8, 1984, p. 5.
4 *Ibid.*
5 *Albany Democrat-Herald*, May 11, 1984, p. 1.

Chapter 8
1 *The Capital Journal*, December 14, 1979, p. 5.
2 *Statesman Journal*, December 14, 1979, p. 3.

Chapter 9
1 *Statesman Journal*, February 2, 1980, p. 2.
2 *Ibid.*, p. 12.
3 *Ibid.*
4 *Ibid.*
5 *Statesman Journal*, February 3, 1980, p. 1.

Chapter 10
1 *Corvallis Gazette-Times*, November 12, 1987, p. 3.

Chapter 12
1 *Statesman Journal*, October 27, 1992, p. 2.

Chapter 14
1 *Albany Democrat-Herald*, July 13, 1999, p. 1.
2 *Corvallis Gazette Times*, March 30, 2000, p. 1.
3 *Ibid.*

Chapter 15
1 *The World*, June 15, 1988, p. 10.

Chapter 18
1 *Statesman Journal*, November 20, 1985, p. 1.
2 *Ibid.*
3 *Ibid.*
4 *Statesman Journal*, January 20, 1994, p. 12.

Chapter 19
1 *Statesman Journal*, July 29, 1989, p. 1.
2 *Statesman Journal*, June 15, 1990, p. 5.

Chapter 20
1 *Corvallis Gazette-Times*, May 10, 1983, p. 2.
2 *Corvallis Gazette-Times*, May 27, 1983, p. 5.
3 *The World*, May 12, 1983, p. 3.
4 *Statesman Journal*, May 25, 1983, p. 1.
5 *Corvallis Gazette-Times*, May 26, 1983, p. 5.

Chapter 23
1 *Eugene Register Guard*, October 3, 2009, p. 1.
2 *Ibid.*
3 *Ibid.*, p. 2.
4 *Ibid.*

Chapter 26
1 *Statesman Journal*, December 22, 1984, p. 5.

Chapter 27
1 *Statesman Journal*, June 24, 1984, p. 1.
2 *Statesman Journal*, June 1, 2008, p. 1.
3 *Ibid.*
4 *Ibid.*
5 *Statesman Journal*, July 16, 2008, p. 2.
6 *Ibid.*
7 Gustafson, A., *Statesman Journal*, January 21, 2010, p. 1.

Chapter 28
1 *The Capital Journal*, August 9, 1977, p. 15.
2 *Statesman Journal*, August 13, 1977, p. 2.
3 *Albany Democrat-Herald*, August 12, 1977, p. 7.
4 Kramer, L., *Corvallis Gazette-Times*, August 10, 1977, p. 1.
5 *Statesman Journal*, August 13, 1977, p. 1.
6 *Corvallis Gazette-Times*, March 16, 1991, p. 4.
7 *Albany Democrat-Herald*, July 22, 1994, p. 1.
8 *Ibid.*
9 *Albany Democrat-Herald*, June 1, 1995, p. 1.
10 *Statesman Journal*, May 14, 1995, p. 1.
11 Davies, J., *Statesman Journal*, October 18, 1995, p. 5.

Chapter 29
1 Gustafson, A., *Statesman Journal*, January 20, 1990, p. 1.
2 *Statesman Journal*, August 15, 1993.

Chapter 31
1 *Mail Tribune*, April 18, 2014, p. 1.
2 *Ibid.*, p. 6.

Bibliography

Albany Democrat-Herald, February 2, 1973; August 12, 1977; December 30, 1982; May 8, 1984; May 11, 1984; February 1, 1985; August 5, 1985; October 3, 1989; July 22, 1994; June 1, 1995; July 13, 1999.

Corvallis Gazette-Times, May 10, 1983; May 26, 1983; May 27, 1983; October 14, 1984; January 22, 1985; January 23, 1985; January 31, 1985; November 12, 1987; March 16, 1991; March 30, 2000.

Davies, J., *Statesman Journal*, October 18, 1995.

Eugene Register Guard, October 3, 2009.

Evenson, J., *Statesman Journal*, March 27, 1982; July 24, 1982; July 27, 1982; July 28, 1982; July 29, 1982; August 5, 1982; August 6, 1982.

Gustafson, A., *Statesman Journal*, January 20, 1990; January 21, 2010.

Hawkins, J., *The Capital Journal*, March 2, 1973.

Jackson, S. P., *Statesman Journal*, March 23, 1990.

Kramer, L., *Corvallis Gazette-Times*, August 10, 1977.

Lipka, M., *Statesman Journal*, December 5, 1982.

MacDonald, J., *The Province*, March 14, 1982.

Mail Tribune, April 18, 2014.

Mulady, K., *The Sacramento Bee*, March 2, 1988.

Postrel, D., *Statesman Journal*, July 17, 1988.

Santa Cruz Sentinel, March 28, 1988.

Shephard, R., *The World*, March 2, 1973.

Spokane Chronicle, April 19, 1984.

Statesman Journal, August 13, 1977; August 13, 1977; December 14, 1979; February 2, 1980; February 3, 1980; April 10, 1980; February 23, 1982; February 24, 1982; November 11, 1982; May 25, 1983; June 24, 1984; December 22, 1984; November 20, 1985; December 25, 1986; February 10, 1987; July 29, 1989; September 16, 1989; September 21, 1989; June 15, 1990; July 15, 1991; October 27, 1992; August 15, 1993; January 20, 1994; May 14, 1995; June 1, 2008; July 16, 2008.

The Capital Journal, August 9, 1977; December 14, 1979.

The Napa Valley Register, August 25, 1987.

The Sacramento Bee, March 23, 1988; September 28, 1989.

The World, May 12, 1983; June 15, 1988.